tortoises & tumbleweeds

JOURNEY THROUGH AN AFRICAN KITCHEN

to my parents, dennis and Lynette barLing,
who Lived Long and travelled far and wide,
but who Loved africa best of all.

Lannice Snyman

Tortoises & Tumbleweeds

Journey through an african kitchen

design by petaldesign
food photography by warren heath
food styling by tamsin snyman

contents

the african table is inspired by ingredients that are close at hand rather than flown in from distant lands. food from the veld and vegetable patch; fish from the sea; and the freshest goodies offered at neighbourhood farmers' markets.

introduction

on my doorstep an undiscovered culinary
wealth waited patiently to be savoured. so
i set about exploring the continent of my birth,
researching its culinary history and writing
and publishing books that nodded to africa.

I was eight in 1956 when my parents headed off for
Algeria in their 'strawberry jelly', a 1947 De Soto
Suburban. They were competing in the third trans-
African rally, and the first (and last) south-to-north race
from the Cape to Cairo. Troubles in Africa put paid to
subsequent events like this.

They faced a gruelling 8 550 miles driving the oldest
car in the race that had already clocked up over 100 000
miles and weighed a whopping 6 000 pounds fully-loaded
with extra water, spares, desert and bush equipment, a
typewriter (mom kept a minute-by-minute diary when she
wasn't behind the wheel), a paraffin stove (for warming
tinned baked beans and bully beef), and her pink umbrella
for the midday sun. Some years earlier they had journeyed
through the Unites States and Canada, so the De Soto had
seen a fair bit of tarmac (and dust-roads) in its time.

My sisters and I were bundled into boarding school
and, for the next year, pretty much faced the world alone.
Our grandparents visited occasionally from Montagu,
bringing snippets of information about how 'the crazy
tumbleweeds' were faring. The odd phone-call from
somewhere in the wilds of Africa was the only link
we had with the intrepid travellers.

When they returned (their badly battered car was shipped back later), they enthralled us with hair-raising tales of their exhausting journey, the countries they had visited and the people they had met. On Sunday nights friends would gather in the lounge, dad would beam his slides onto a huge screen, and we relived the expedition together. I had never been further from Cape Town than Swellendam; now the whole continent of Africa opened up to me in the most up-close-and-personal way.

When, years later, a career in food claimed my heart, soul and future, childhood memories of African tales continued to colour my vision. While most South African cooks and food writers of the seventies, eighties and nineties explored any and every voguish cuisine of the time – as long as it wasn't local – I continued to be drawn to my own Anglo-Saxon-African roots.

Books, magazines and restaurant menus tripped gaily through France, the Mediterranean and the Orient. 'Tex-Mex' fired up our palates, pens, and wooden spoons. We were led astray by flavours as obscure (to Africa) as Californian, modern British, multi-directional Australian, and seductive Thai.

On my doorstep an undiscovered culinary wealth waited patiently to be savoured. So I set about exploring the continent of my birth, researching its culinary history and writing and publishing books that nodded to Africa. The most important, *Rainbow Cuisine* was launched in 1998 after many years spent journeying to every accessible (and some seemingly inaccessible) part of the country; trips that introduced me to cooks of all colours and creeds, bridged a host of culinary divides and enriched and enthralled me. *Tortoises & Tumbleweeds* is a sequel to that book, illustrating a true foodie's love of continuing a life-long, soul-enriching journey of discovery.

Our diverse cultural and culinary history means that we filch ideas freely from those who make up our rainbow nation, as well as from neighbouring countries and the Indian Ocean islands. The trick is to put it all into the melting potjie, flavour it deftly, and imbue our creation with a personal stamp of finesse.

Recipes, however, should honour the folk who created them and the land that provides the ingredients. *Tortoises & Tumbleweeds* maintains this synergy by setting the food against the beauty of South Africa's scenic splendour.

As a food writer I track trends and challenge predictability; glance over my shoulder while looking to the future. What inspires me is that sharing food – a simple snack, a casual campfire repast, or a banquet – is a powerful and intimate form of communication. My life has been richly blessed with such occasions.

Those of us at the helm of South African cuisine are duty-bound to continue exploring, fine-tuning and publishing our inheritance. Happily, there's a growing market of temptable palates out there, including tourists and home cooks hungry to discover what they've been missing out on all these years.

Recipes in this book are inspired by early cookbooks and folk who opened their hearts, homes and huts and shared their culinary vision. Some remain true to their origins; others reflect a merging of ideas; many are rooted in the mists of time; all have been updated for the modern kitchen. Happily, none include tortoises, which are protected now and no longer simmered into soup.

All recapture memorable food moments and the feeling of love that I experienced as a child when enjoying lunch around the family table. Let *Tortoises & Tumbleweeds* take you on your own culinary journey through an African kitchen. Enjoy!

a kaleidoscope of colours, creeds and social backgrounds makes up the south african nation, creating an extraordinarily complex society and a patchwork of lifestyles and food styles.

Some have dwelt here since the mists of time; many came from far-flung corners of the globe to make their home at the southern tip of Africa. All have their roots buried deep in the African soil.

Our place in the larger global village has been wrought by the tenacity of hunter-gatherers, migratory pastoralists and pioneers who survived in a harsh terrain and a troubled political and social arena.

Though South Africa has only recently begun to take its place as a gastronomic destination among countries with more famous cuisines, it was probably in Africa that man began, and where he learnt to master fire, without which cooking and survival would have been improbable.

San (known as Bushmen), South Africa's oldest residents, are true children of nature. They have lived off land and sea since the Stone Age, subsisting in areas which, due to the advance of both whites and blacks, continue to shrink in size. The few remaining scatterlings of this ancient tribe cling to their past with an ever-decreasing degree of success. Few men now hunt with bows and arrows. Few women gather food from the desert, scrub and fynbos.

Khoikhoi, the San's successor (European settlers called them Hottentots), were also hunter-gatherers who learned to herd cattle and fat-tailed sheep. They formed a loose society with the San and lived in the rich grazing lands of the southern Cape coastal regions. However, their wandering lifestyle and lack of hereditary chieftainship created a fragile social infrastructure. Settler expansion, drought, disease and livestock theft took their toll. Traditional ways of life died out, and eventually they were absorbed into the rest of the population. Anthropologists coined the name Khoisan as a term to embrace the San and Khoi, who were of common stock.

The unhurried path of black pastoralists to the south from the Congo basin in the region of the Great Lakes of central East Africa took several centuries, a journey governed by geographic, social and political dictates.

Tribes split in several directions, some remaining in the interior, others filtering down the east coast. Despite shared roots, clans developed in isolation, and formed several broad ethnic groups, each retaining its own cultural identity, language and traditional ways of cooking. They finally came into contact and conflict with the Khoisan, with each other and, inevitably, with Europeans on their own treks inland from the Cape Colony.

opposite, top left: *Roasted masala is freshly ground with a pestle and mortar to add flavour to traditional dishes.*
opposite, top right: *Xhosa women in traditional dress with their faces decorated with daubs of white clay.*
opposite, bottom: *There are many different types of high-energy Zulu dances which are often boisterous and illustrate various aspects of tribal life.*

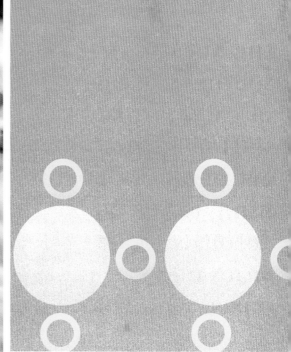

THE NDEBELE IN
SOUTHERN AREAS
OF GAUTENG ARE
SKILLED IN THE
ART OF BEADWORK
USING BRIGHTLY-
COLOURED GLASS
BEADS OFTEN
MIXED WITH WIRE.

Our knowledge of the way of life of early African man has been gleaned from word of mouth as well as ancient middens and the rock art of the San, who painted scenes of life, death and survival on walls of caves in many parts of southern Africa.

Snippets of written information come from Portuguese sailors who called at the Cape coast during the sixteenth century. They were on voyages of discovery, spurred on by trade and the search for gold, precious stones, ivory, amber and spices. They told of Strandlopers (also called Watermen, outcasts from the Khoikhoi community), who collected seafood and built stone traps to snare fish as the tide receded. They also described the lifestyle of black hunters, herders and cultivators, telling of rich pastures, and of success in tilling and planting.

They wrote of millet (indigenous to Africa and Asia), 'white and the size of peppercorns' being pounded into flour between stones for cakes which were baked in the embers of fires. They described how millet was fermented for beer and strained through birds' nests. They mentioned crops such as melons, beans, gourds and sugar cane known as 'sweet cane'.

This was the primitive culinary inheritance of Jan van Riebeeck, who was sent to the Cape by the Dutch East India Company in 1652 to establish a refreshment station for ships plying the sea route between West and East. He found a lifestyle of people to whom food was a matter of survival, rather than a creative art form.

The new South Africans quickly learned skills from indigenous peoples who had mastered the art of survival. They bartered for sustenance, learned to hunt and fish, and gathered wild plants for food and medicinal purposes. From these humble, shared foundations grew a fascinating, extraordinarily complex cuisine.

Left: *A Ndebele lady sits on her mat, patiently creating a masterpiece of beadwork which will be offered for sale to tourists at roadside markets and craft galleries in the cities.*

Holland ruled the Cape of Good Hope for about 150 years, during which time European elements were added to indigenous African cuisine. Dutch cooking was influenced by Holland's colonies, which had access to ingredients such as rice, and gentle spices like nutmeg and cinnamon. Their fondness for lavish quantities of butter added richness and stodginess that distinguishes Cape Dutch recipes.

Convicts from China and slaves from Mozambique joined the cosmopolitan community in the shadow of Table Mountain. From 1667, Malay slaves and political exiles were brought from Java, core of the colonial Dutch East Indies, and other Indonesian islands. They were fine artisans, fishermen, seamstresses, tailors and basket-makers – and excellent cooks – whose skills were appreciated by their European masters.

Their impact on the Cape table was profound. They refined what was already in place, added Eastern nuances, and made excellent use of local ingredients from land and sea. Their unique cooking skills were summed up by C Louis Leipoldt, author and connoisseur of early Cape cookery: 'The outstanding characteristics are the free, almost heroic, use of spices and aromatic flavourings, the prolonged, steady but slow application of moist heat to meat dishes, and the skillful blending of many diverse constituents into a combination that still holds the essential goodness of each.'

The Malays brought spices from home and introduced the pleasure of combining sweet and sour and multi-flavoured masalas. Spicy sambals, chutneys and pickles perked up palates more familiar with bland European fare.

French culinary finesse was introduced in the late 1600s with the arrival of a small group of French Huguenots – Protestant refugees in search of religious freedom. They influenced our cuisine through their appreciation of fruit and confitures (jams and preserves which we call konfyt). They were selected for their skills in 'cultivating the vine' and settled along the Berg River, in Drakenstein and De Olifantshoek, later known as Franschhoek. The entire region would later be known as the Cape winelands, which produces New World wines and where many villages, streets and towns are named after their original French founders.

In the late 1700s Britain assumed rulership of the Cape and introduced a distinctive colonial lifestyle. French and Danish ships stopped in, as did vessels from other European ports and from the United States of America.

ABOVE: *Dried beans are a menu cornerstone for many families. Here packets are displayed by a Cape Malay shopkeeper ready for cooking into nourishing meals.*

Yet another milestone in human terms occurred in 1920 – an influx of British settlers brought to augment the white population on the troubled eastern frontier. Their culinary contribution to our table included pies, hot puddings and roast meats.

Thirty years later German soldiers of the disbanded Anglo-German Legion were resettled here. Many later relocated to what is now Namibia, but some chose to remain in South Africa. Their love of wurst (sausage) and hearty casseroles added yet another dimension to our menus.

Threads of the tapestry of South Africa's cuisine continued to be woven together. An influx of Mauritians

came to what was then called Natal. Indians were brought there in the mid-1800s to work on sugar cane farms. Indian dishes – notably curries – were introduced. Initially ingredients were imported; later the settlement grew its own rice, chillies, ginger, cumin, coriander and garlic, but continued to bring tamarind, black pepper, mace, nutmeg, saffron and coconut from the East.

The discovery of gold along the Witwatersrand in the Transvaal Republic in 1886 attracted not only investment from Britain, America and Germany, but also mineworkers, businessmen and professionals from these countries, as well as from Australia and eastern Europe.

In the ensuing years more and more people became attracted to the sunny South African lifestyle, enriching the country with their own knowledge, culture and culinary traditions.

As for present trends and future predictions of South African cooking, the story continues to unfold. With urbanization and the demise of apartheid came a re-evaluation of long-fragmented traditions. Urban blacks have adopted aspects of Western diet at the expense of indigenous ingredients and traditional dishes and cooking methods. Frying, for example, has usurped the time-honoured roasting of meat, maize meal is bought in packets and no longer ground between two stones, and the younger generation seldom asks its elders for advice on the foods of times gone by.

Whites, meanwhile, are looking to their roots with renewed interest and embracing the ingredients, recipes and cooking techniques favoured by black communities. Dishes like pap (maize meal porridge), umngqusho (samp and beans), mopane worms and morogo (a variety of wild greens) are crossing the black/white divide. Home cooks, food writers and chefs are rethinking their inherited culinary ethic and merging our myriad styles into a harmonious, yet multifaceted, whole.

Food-savvy tourists who visit our shores will find much on the South African table that bears testimony to all who comprise the complex rainbow nation.

LEFT: *Snoek fishermen return to Hout Bay harbour after a successful day fishing in the chilly waters off Cape Point.*

ABOVE: *A farmer brings a trolley of spring onions and fresh salad greens to sell at the market.*

Breakfast may be as simple as a rusk dunked in a mug of coffee, as homely as a bowl of porridge, or as healthy as juicy, sun-ripened fruit.

Breakfast
CHAPTER TWO

A SOUTH AFRICAN BREAKFAST may be simple or elaborate, homely or wildly extravagant. For those who can't resist going the whole hog, a hearty cooked breakfast is hard to resist. The line-up starts with eggs and bacon; extras include grilled tomatoes and fried mushrooms, as well as boerewors, chops and steak for those who must have meat.

Long ago, breakfast in rural black homes was a bowl of power-packed amasi (curdled milk). Later, when cereal crops were cultivated, porridge with amasi or milk and honey became the breakfast of choice. Though made from a wide variety of grains, including sorghum and millet (sadly no longer readily available), maize meal porridge (called pap) was the most popular of all, and remains so to this day.

As in the past, rural cooking of maize meal is still done in clay pots over open fires, while practiced hands twirl stirring sticks to an ancient rhythm. The consistency varies from clan to clan. For example, VhaVenda women in Limpopo near the border of Zimbabwe ladle mukonde (king's porridge) onto flat wooden dishes. The layers form a pyramid as they set. And, in some communities, women demonstrate their affection for their husbands by intricately patterning his maize meal with a corn husk.

While breakfasts have become more cosmopolitan, traditional dishes like frikkadels, sosaties and skilpadjies (liver wrapped in caul fat) still pop up on morning menus. In coastal towns there are fresh oysters, black mussels, fishcakes, smoorsnoek and poached haddock to be had. In trout-farming areas, fresh or smoked trout is a highlight.

Regional recipes are a treat, like the Hantam speciality of stone-ground boermeel (farmer's meal) porridge studded with raisins which, in days past were bartered from travelling Jewish smouse (peddlers). You may also be offered toast spread with kambrokonfyt (kambro jam), made from the roots of potato-like tubers found nowhere else in the country.

Weather permitting, breakfast is served outdoors on urban stoeps and patios, in sandy beach coves and leafy country gardens. In game reserves, visitors are treated to an early-morning meal in a dry river bed with nothing but wild expanses of untamed veld all around.

putupap

Slow, steady heat is important when making this basic porridge, as is the traditional stirring stick, which takes different forms in different black clans. If you don't have one, a wooden spoon will do.

serves 4

750ml water
250ml milk
5ml salt
150g maize meal
30g butter
125ml cream or milk
extra butter and honey, to serve

Bring the water and milk to the boil in a medium saucepan with the salt. Slowly stir in the maize meal, whisking briskly to prevent lumps forming. Cover and simmer over very low heat for 15 minutes, stirring occasionally. Mix in the butter and cream or milk.

Serve hot, topped with a block of butter and a drizzle of honey; they will melt into the porridge as you eat it.

maize rice and mabele pap

This porridge of malt-flavoured grain sorghum (amabele or mabele) and maize rice (crushed dried corn) is a favourite of the Swazi and Tswana people. It has a wonderfully nutty flavour and rough texture.

serves 4

125ml maize rice
500ml water, plus extra for soaking
250ml milk
5ml salt
125ml grain sorghum (Maltabella)
milk and brown sugar, to serve

Tip the maize rice into a bowl, add plenty of cold water to cover generously and set aside for at least 8 hours to soak. Drain.

Bring the water and milk to the boil in a medium saucepan with the salt. Stir in the maize rice and grain sorghum, cover and simmer over very low heat for 15 minutes, stirring occasionally.

Serve hot with milk and brown sugar.

PRE-PACKAGED MAIZE MEAL IS WIDELY AVAILABLE, SO THE TIME-HONOURED ART OF GRINDING MAIZE BETWEEN TWO STONES HAS ALL BUT DIED OUT. BUT PURISTS STILL MAINTAIN THAT HAND-GROUND MEAL MAKES THE BEST PORRIDGE OF ALL.

CRUMPETS WITH BERRIES, YOGHURT AND HONEY

Crumpets (also known as flapjacks) are a favourite British tea-time treat, buttered and served with honey or jam. They're bliss for breakfast with berries and yoghurt. Crumpets are best served straight from the pan, but the batter may be prepared several hours in advance. Keep chilled in the meanwhile.

SERVES 5 TO 6

150g cake flour
10ml baking powder
1ml salt
30ml castor sugar
15ml melted butter
1 egg, lightly beaten
60ml buttermilk
125ml milk
vegetable oil
berries, plain yoghurt and honey, to serve

Sift together the flour, baking powder, salt and castor sugar in a bowl. Lightly mix together the melted butter, egg, buttermilk and milk. Mix into the dry ingredients to form a smooth, thickish batter.

Heat a little oil in a frying pan, drop in spoonfuls of batter and cook the crumpets until golden and surface bubbles pop. Flip over and cook the other side. Drain on kitchen paper.

Arrange the crumpets on a serving plate or individual plates, and serve with berries, yoghurt and honey.

SWEETCORN FRITTERS

African corn recipes are as old as the hills. Plants were taken to Europe from America following the travels of Columbus; Portuguese seafarers brought it to Africa at the start of the sixteenth century. It was called 'milho' from which the word 'mealie' is derived. Traditionalists use chopped corn kernels sliced from the cobs for these fritters; a tin of cream-style sweetcorn is much more convenient. The uncooked mixture tends to get runny, so mix it shortly before frying the fritters.

SERVES 8

340g tin cream-style sweetcorn
1 egg, lightly beaten
5ml dijon mustard
125ml cake flour
2ml baking powder
1ml grated nutmeg
salt and milled black pepper
vegetable oil

Mix together the sweetcorn, egg and mustard in a bowl. Sift in the flour and baking powder, season with nutmeg and a little salt and pepper, and mix well.

Make eight corn cakes: fry spoonfuls of the batter in hot oil in a frying pan until crisp on both sides and cooked right through. If insufficiently cooked, the fritters will be runny in the middle. Drain well on kitchen paper, then arrange on a hot plate. Serve warm.

HERB-ROASTED tomatoes

Tomatoes flavoured with fresh herbs are wonderful with sweetcorn fritters or eggs and bacon. The nice thing is that cooking time isn't all that critical – the tomatoes will quite happily languish in the warmer until you're ready for them.

serves 6 to 8

6 large roma tomatoes

60ml chopped herbs (parsley, basil, oregano)

olive oil

salt and milled black pepper

sugar

Heat the oven to 200°C. Slice the tomatoes in half horizontally and place in a baking dish. Scatter with herbs and drizzle over a little olive oil. Season with salt, pepper and sugar, and roast for about 20 minutes. Switch on the oven griller for a few minutes to brown them. Transfer to a serving dish and serve warm.

sweetcorn fritters and herb-roasted tomatoes are delicious together for breakfast.

I DISCOVERED BOTH THESE
LONG-FORGOTTEN RECIPES
IN AN OLD COOKBOOK AND
BROUGHT THEM TO LIFE
FOR NEW GENERATIONS
TO ENJOY.

eggs in tomatoes

The English are partial to bacon, eggs and tomato for breakfast, and this is the way British travellers in the 'outposts of the Empire' started their day while on safari in the wilds of Africa in the 1930s and 1940s.

serves 4

4 large tomatoes
salt and milled black pepper
4 eggs, at room temperature
250ml soft white or brown breadcrumbs
30ml chopped parsley
8 rashers rindless bacon
vegetable oil

Heat the oven to 200°C. Cut a slice off the top of each tomato and remove the pith and seeds. Season the cavities with salt and pepper and set aside to drain, cut side down.

Soft-boil the eggs: place in a small saucepan and add cold water to cover. Bring to the boil, boil for 1 minute, then switch off the heat and allow to stand for 2 minutes. Stir occasionally to keep the yolks in the middle.

Lift the eggs from the water, plunge into cold water to cool a bit, then remove the shells. Pop the eggs into the tomatoes and place in a baking dish with the tomato 'lids'.

Mix together the crumbs and parsley, and season with salt and pepper. Sprinkle onto the tomatoes and bake for 10 minutes. Meanwhile, fry the bacon in a little oil in a frying pan. Serve the eggs piping hot with bacon alongside.

mushrooms in sherry

Mushrooms once grew wild on the slopes of Table Mountain and on the Cape Flats where German farmers established vegetable farms in the late 1800s. They're heaven for breakfast, especially when simply prepared without too many ingredients to mask their glorious flavour and texture.

serves 4 to 6

6 large black or brown mushrooms
50g butter
2 garlic cloves, crushed
30ml finely sliced sage leaves
salt and milled black pepper
125ml medium dry sherry
30ml chopped parsley

Wipe the mushrooms with a damp cloth or rinse, gills down, under running water.

Heat the butter in a large frying pan. When it's sizzling, add the garlic and mushrooms, gills down, and fry for 2 to 3 minutes.

Flip them over. Scatter over the sage, season with salt and pepper, and pour in the sherry. Cover and simmer for a few minutes until the mushroom stalks are tender when pierced with a toothpick.

Transfer the mushrooms to a warm plate. Add the parsley to the pan juices and boil uncovered until slightly reduced and thickened. Spoon over the mushrooms and serve hot on toast or with fried eggs, bacon and tomato.

kedgeree

England's colonisation of India spawned a host of Anglo-Indian fusion dishes that subsequently graced the Victorian table. From there it was only a short hop to Africa. Kedgeree – haddock, rice and hard-boiled eggs – is just one such recipe that survived all the globetrotting.

serves 6

500ml water

2 bay leaves, plus extra for garnishing

10 black peppercorns

300g haddock

80g butter

1 onion, chopped

small knob green ginger, peeled and grated

5ml curry powder

2ml turmeric

5ml salt

milled black pepper

250ml uncooked basmati rice

60ml cream

lemon juice

2 hard-boiled eggs, shelled and quartered

Bring the water to the boil in a wide saucepan with the bay leaves and peppercorns. Add the haddock, cover and poach very gently (the liquid should barely move) until cooked. Thin fillets will take about 6 minutes; plumper steaks require a few minutes longer.

Drain the fish, remove and discard the skin (this is easiest to do while it's still hot), and roughly flake the flesh. Strain 375ml of the poaching liquid into a measuring jug.

Heat the butter in a medium saucepan and fry the onion until golden. Add the ginger, curry powder, turmeric, salt and pepper, and stir for about 15 seconds to sizzle the spices. Stir in the rice, then add the poaching liquid. Cover and simmer for about 15 minutes until all the liquid has been absorbed and the rice is cooked. Mix in the haddock and cream, flavour with a squeeze of lemon juice, and heat through.

Serve the kedgeree directly from the pan, or transfer to a warm serving dish. Garnish with quartered hard-boiled eggs and a few bay leaves for a bit of colour.

kedgeree was originally served for breakfast but it's equally good for a casual family supper.

scrambled eggs with smoked fish

I discovered this super scramble in a late eighteenth-century manuscript. In those days a wide variety of eggs were enjoyed, including penguin eggs and eggs from wild ducks, peahens, turkeys, geese, ostriches and guinea fowls. Turtle and tortoise eggs were sometimes to be had too. Any smoked fish would be good, including haddock, smoked trout and – if money's no object – smoked salmon.

serves 4

200g smoked fish
6 eggs
60ml cream
15ml chopped thyme leaves
salt and milled black pepper
butter and vegetable oil
1 onion, sliced
chopped parsley, for garnishing

Fillet and skin the fish and break into small pieces ('mootjies' in local parlance). Lightly whisk together the eggs and cream in a bowl, add the thyme and season with salt and pepper.

Heat a generous amount of butter and a dash of oil in a frying pan, and fry the onion until golden. Stir in the fish and egg mixture. Cook over very gentle heat, stirring constantly, until almost set but still creamy. Garnish with chopped parsley.

Make sure everyone is ready and waiting; scrambled eggs should be served as soon as they're done.

LOBSTERS, LINEFISH
& NEW WORLD WINES

CAPE PENINSULA & BOLAND

OCEANS, MOUNTAINS AND VINEYARDS FORM AN ENCHANTING BACKDROP TO THE SOUTHERN CAPE, WHERE THERE'S A WONDERFUL SYNERGY BETWEEN WORK AND PLAY; UPBEAT CITY LIVING AND TRANQUIL COUNTRY PURSUITS.

On the Cape table – South Africa's culinary heartland – are foods from sea and farmland, accompanied by the finest New World wines.

This part of the world was once called the Cape of Storms and dramatic changing seasons play an important part in setting food fashions apart from the rest of the subcontinent. Spring, summer, autumn, winter – each in its own unique way – heralds new crops and different menu ideas.

Elsewhere rain falls in summer; here winter downpours soak lands that provide fruit and vegetables. Wild mushrooms grow in forests when rain and sun have worked their magic; waterblommetjies bloom in dams for winter bredies; berries ripen in early summer for tarts and jam. Peaches, nectarines, plums, grapes, pears and apples ripen in sun-dappled orchards.

Unlike landlocked provinces to the north, currents of two oceans – the warm Mozambique of the Indian; the icy Benguela of the Atlantic – sweep past the Cape Peninsula, impacting on weather, crops and the migration of fish.

Seafoods are an integral part of Cape menus, and no-one knows more than born-and-bred Kaapenaars (Capetonians) about the delights of fresh fish braaiing over open coals, crayfish simmering seductively in a pot, perlemoen (abalone) steaks sizzling in butter, and freshly-gathered black mussels spilling their ambrosial juices into a mix of onion, wine and herbs.

Sports fishermen try their luck for geelbek, kob, red steenbras, roman, stumpnose, steenbras and the elusive galjoen – our national fish which is named after the stately Spanish sailing vessel. The summer gamefish season attracts anglers from all over the world to troll for tuna, yellowtail and marlin in the waters off Cape Point.

Fishermen eagerly anticipate the snoek season in late winter. Instinct and financial reward guide their lines, as efforts to track migratory patterns of shoals have long escaped logic. Snoek are braaied, smoked, pickled and made into smoorsnoek, a spicy mélange of fish and rice.

Cape Town, the 'mother city', is sheltered in a natural bowl formed by the grand backdrop of Devil's Peak, Lion's Head and Table Mountain, 1087 metres high and 150 million years old. In the olden days a flagstaff was erected on the pinnacle and fires were lit to signal the arrival of ships – and hungry sailors – in Table Bay. Distant West Coast farmers would hastily round up livestock and crops and bring them to town to sell at the markets.

The hospitality of the Tavern of the Seas, as the city became known, started in 1652, when Jan van Riebeeck, our first 'inn keeper' planted his famous vegetable garden to feed passing seafarers. Fresh drinking water was abundant, and fruit and vegetable crops flourished.

Wild herbs and lemon and peach leaves flavoured early Cape dishes. Non-indigenous dried spices were brought from the East; salt was collected from the Salt River.

After slaves were brought from Java and the Indonesian islands, Malay eating houses appeared on the scene, attracting portly burghers, seamen and soldiers of the garrison, who tucked into inexpensive, spicy meals.

Many Cape Malays still reside in the Bo-Kaap, also called the Malay Quarter, on the slopes of Signal Hill on the city's fringe. The area has been declared a national monument, and picturesque streets are lined with spruced-up dwellings, many still owned by descendants of the original inhabitants.

Though early wine-making endeavours were charged more by enthusiasm than expertise, vines were imported for Constantia's historical farms of Groot Constantia, Klein Constantia, Bergvliet, Hoop van Constantia, Buitenverwachting, Alphen and Constantia Uitsig.

TOP LEFT: *Cape Malays still live in the Bo-Kaap in the Cape Town city bowl, as they have for centuries.*
TOP RIGHT: *A picture-perfect view of Table Mountain and the Twelve Apostles which overlook Camps Bay.*
BOTTOM RIGHT: *The V&A Waterfront encompasses a bustling working harbour with magnificently restored buildings, bringing to life the architectural character of a bygone era.*

CAPE TOWN, THE 'MOTHER CITY', IS SHELTERED IN A NATURAL BOWL FORMED BY THE GRAND BACKDROP OF DEVIL'S PEAK, LION'S HEAD AND TABLE MOUNTAIN.

today cape town and the winelands attract international visitors to wine, dine and relax in glorious surroundings at gourmet restaurants, sophisticated hotels, charming guest houses and homely inns.

The Cape's first success was a fortified wine which emulated the fashionable tipple of Holland and England. Soon 'sweet, luscious and excellent wines' were being snaffled up by Europe's royalty and the upper crust of its society, and travellers flocked to the Cape to experience them first hand. During the halcyon days of the nineteenth century, the lush Constantia valley was the social centre of the colony, and high society life consisted of picnics, luncheons and all-day shooting parties.

Following the tracks of antelope on their seasonal migrations, settlers – followed by Voortrekkers – ventured inland through spectacular mountain passes, where rocks still bear the scars of ox wagon wheels. By the end of the century the Boland was flourishing, the famous Cape winelands had been planted, and charming towns like Stellenbosch, Franschhoek, Paarl and Drakenstein were established.

Today Cape Town and the winelands attract international visitors to wine, dine and relax in glorious surroundings at gourmet restaurants, sophisticated hotels, charming guest houses and homely inns. Menus boast fresh local produce from fish and vegetable markets; winelists include acclaimed local wines as well as labels from other New World producers and classics from European estates.

opposite, left: *Historical Vergelegen Wine Estate in Somerset West was originally granted to Willem Adriaan van der Stel, Governor of the Cape, in 1700.*
opposite, top right: *The legendary Vin de Constance sweet wine, sought after by kings and emperors in the eighteenth and nineteenth centuries, was revived in 1986 by the Jooste family at Klein Constantia Estate.*
opposite, centre: *Vines in the eary morning sun at Constantia Uitsig Wine Estate.*
opposite, bottom right: *Le Quartier Français in Franschhoek is an exclusive auberge with two restaurants, ICI and The Tasting Room, which has several times been named as one of the 50 Best Restaurants in the World.*

Like harbours around the world, Table Bay, as well as the bay at Simon's Town – previously known as Yzelstein Bay – has many fascinating stories to tell about vessels driven by sail, paddle, screw and steam, which found shelter here. Brigs and schooners berthed with bags of coffee from Brazil, and sugar and spices from the East; ships set sail for tropical seas and southern ice floes, and for naval expeditions and maritime wars. Less illustrious visitors included convict ships and whalers en route to southern whaling grounds to satisfy the world's need for soap, margarine and oil.

These same docks welcomed entrepreneurs who arrived from all parts of the globe after gold and diamonds were discovered in the interior; bade farewell to soldiers during two world wars – and welcomed them home. Today, Table Bay hosts luxurious ocean liners, sleek sailing ships and fancy yachts from many far-flung ports.

The area has been transformed into the Victoria & Alfred Waterfront, a development of huge historical and commercial significance, encompassing a bustling working harbour as well as meticulously restored buildings predating the turn of the last century. Ferries take tourists to visit Robben Island, where Nelson Mandela was imprisioned. There are shops, restaurants and luxury hotels abound, the kaleidoscope of boats, barges and swooping, shrieking seabirds echoing the scene that has welcomed seafarers for more than three centuries.

The pleasures of Cape cuisine have spread to the rest of the country as well as to other countries in Africa, although Capetonians insist that it's best enjoyed here where it began, close to its roots and the sights and sounds of the folk who made it great.

In terms of hospitality the Tavern of the Seas has come a long way. Although early Malay 'cook-shops' are but a fond memory, many restaurants have taken their place, some featuring local cuisine, many owned, managed and cheffed by fascinating folk from near and far, whose expertise has broadened our culinary landscape even more. Dining at the Cape provides the gourmet with a world of food on one many-flavoured plate.

DROËWORS (DRIED SAUSAGE) IS A FAVOURITE SNACK WHICH IS MADE FROM BOEREWORS.

IT IS SOLD IN FARMERS' MARKETS AND AT SOME SPECIALIST DELI'S.

snacks, starters & soups

CHAPTER FOUR

africans enjoy simple snacks and starters, and unsophisticated soups. Rather than cook complicated recipes, we prefer to plump dried mopane worms in a pot of simmering water, or nibble sliced biltong just as early trek-farmers did to allay hunger pangs as they moved from one place to the next.

Coastal dwellers – like the ancient Strandlopers (beach walkers) – do things just as casually, pickling periwinkles, gathering wild oysters at low tide, and plucking black mussels from the rocks, steaming them open in a pan or over the coals, and dipping them in hot garlic butter.

Bokkems are a popular West Coast snack. Small fish like harders are netted and taken to factories for salting ('about three shovelsful of salt for each basket of fish') and drying. Bunches of bokkems hang in local stores and at open-air restaurants, ready to kick off a seafood feast.

Soups are a mélange of whatever seasonal ingredients are at hand rather than studiously composed creations that require weighing, measuring and clarifying to get them just right. They're sustaining and gloriously flavoured, attesting to the skill of the cook rather than the author of the recipe. The broth is sometimes thin, though more often substantial, echoing times when they were thickened with mashed vegetables, flour, rice or egg mixed with a little wine or cream.

Even before Jan van Riebeeck planted his famous vegetable gardens to feed seafarers, herbs and greens like sorrel, wateruintjie (water hawthorn) and wild cabbage and spinach were gathered from the slopes of Table Mountain for soup.

Tortoise soup was prepared with beasties that roamed freely in the countryside. They were boiled in salted water with herbs and spices, then the broth was strained and thickened with tapioca. Lemon juice and wine added flavour, and the meat was stirred back in before serving.

Soup is sometimes made with home-made stock; more often the broth is formed by the patient simmering of meat, fish, vegetables and pulses. Traditional flavourings include a dash of curry powder or nutmeg. Colour comes from saffron or turmeric; in the past leaves of beetroot, spinach and fig did the job.

maize
and nut fritters

These nutty nibbles are a free adaptation of mukhomo, popular in Venda in Limpopo Province ever since groundnuts (peanuts) appeared on the scene. The VhaVenda roast green mealies (sweetcorn) over the coals, pound the kernels with nuts and press it into small cakes. They're great with a chilled beer.

makes about 12; serves 4 to 6

410g tin whole kernel corn
100g roasted and salted peanuts
1 egg, lightly beaten
2ml paprika
salt and milled black pepper
vegetable oil

Drain the corn, then lay on a wad of kitchen paper to blot off all the moisture (if you don't, the fritters will splutter as they fry). Crush with the peanuts to a fairly rough paste. A food processor works well, though pounding with a pestle and mortar is the traditional way of doing it. Mix in the egg, paprika and a little salt and pepper.

Heat oil in a frying pan for shallow frying. Drop in tablespoonfuls of fritter mixture and fry for about a minute on each side until golden and crisp.

Drain on kitchen paper, arrange in a bowl and serve warm or at room temperature.

masala-rubbed patat with dhai

Sweet potatoes (generally called patat) are everybody's favourite spud. Here's a simple way of preparing them which is great for snacks as well as a side dish for meat.

serves 6

750g sweet potatoes
olive oil
15ml Roasted Masala (page 213),
   or Garam Masala (page 214)
Dhai (page 154), for dipping

Heat the oven to 200°C. Wash the sweet potatoes, cut lengthwise into wedges and arrange in a roasting dish. Drizzle generously with olive oil, then sprinkle with roasted masala or garam masala and toss everything together well.

Roast uncovered for about 50 minutes until the potato wedges are tender and beautifully browned. Switch on the oven griller towards the end of the roasting time for extra crustiness and colour if you wish.

Arrange the patat in a bowl and serve warm or cool with dhai to dip them in.

vegetable samoosas

Indian immigrants introduced these crisp and spicy pastries to Africa, and they've been enthusiastically adopted by Cape Malays who fill them with a wide variety of stuffings, including vegetables, lamb, beef, chicken and fish. The origins of this tasty snack-food, however, is ancient Persia (Iraq) and variations can be found throughout the Middle East and Northern African countries including Algeria, Morocco and Liberia. You could make your own pastry, but it's much easier to use pre-made samoosa or spring roll pastry. The uncooked samoosas can be refrigerated for two days, or frozen for three months.

makes 45

vegetable oil	10ml ground cumin
1 onion, finely chopped	5ml curry powder
2 garlic cloves, crushed	5ml Garam Masala (page 214)
2 potatoes, peeled and finely chopped	2ml turmeric
	250ml frozen peas, defrosted
4 carrots, peeled and finely chopped	125ml chopped coriander
5ml salt	15 sheets spring roll pastry
	1 egg white, lightly beaten

Heat a little oil in a medium saucepan and fry the onion until translucent. Add the garlic, potatoes, carrots, salt, cumin, curry powder, garam masala and turmeric. Cover and cook over medium heat for about 5 minutes until the vegetables are tender. Add the peas and coriander and heat through. Allow to cool.

Keep the pastry covered with a damp cloth while making the samoosas. Cut each sheet into three strips. Place about 20ml of the filling at the end of each strip. Fold the pastry over the filling on the diagonal and continue folding to the end of the pastry. Brush the edges with egg white and press firmly with your fingers to seal. Continue until all the pastry and filling have been used up. Layer the samoosas on a tray interleaved with waxed paper as you go.

Deep-fry the samoosas in hot oil until crisp and golden. Drain on kitchen paper. Pile onto a tray and serve warm.

BILTONG

The concept of drying meat isn't the sole preserve of Afrikaners; black tribes dried the flesh of animals. The Swazis call it umcweba or umcwayiba. Coriander seeds, formerly brought from Asia, are a vital ingredient in good biltong. The name is Greek for bedbugs – nasty goggas which the seeds resemble!

makes about 2kg

2,5kg lean meat (beef, venison, ostrich)
60ml coriander seeds
60ml salt
10ml milled black pepper
45ml brown sugar
5ml ground cloves
wine or cider vinegar

Cut the meat into strips about 2cm x 3cm. Roast the coriander in a dry frying pan to bring out the flavour, then crush lightly with a pestle and mortar. Mix in the salt, pepper, brown sugar and cloves.

Sprinkle a little of the spice mixture into a glass dish and top with a layer of meat strips. Sprinkle very lightly with vinegar, and season once more with the spices. Continue in this way until meat and seasoning are used up.

Refrigerate for a day, mixing every couple of hours so the meat flavours evenly. Hang the strips to dry in a suitable spot (in the garage rafters or behind the fridge where there's movement of air). It will take about five days, depending on how dry the weather is, and whether you prefer your biltong dry or slightly moist.

DRYING MEAT AND FISH WAS A METHOD OF PRESERVATION PRIOR TO REFRIGERATION, AND THIS SALTY, SPICY DRIED MEAT IS ONE OF SOUTH AFRICA'S SIGNATURE SNACKS.

puri, dukka and butter bean mash

This snack platter links Africa from south to north: puri are Cape Malay breads; Egyptian dukka is a roughly ground mix of roasted nuts and seeds; butter bean mash salutes the continent's love of pulses. Hazelnuts are the nuts of choice for dukka, though you could substitute macadamias, pistachios or cashews. Other serving ideas include mixing dukka with breadcrumbs and coating chops or fish for frying or braaiing, and sprinkling it over rice, salads and vegetables. Dukka keeps well in a sealed container in the fridge. Butter bean mash may be covered and chilled for a day or two before serving. If you don't wish to make your own puri, any good, crusty bread will do.

serves 6 to 8

Puri (page 190)

DUKKA

50g hazelnuts

50g sesame seeds

30ml cumin seeds

30ml coriander seeds

15ml dried thyme

salt and milled black pepper

BUTTER BEAN MASH

410g tin butter beans, drained

1 garlic clove, crushed (optional)

1ml ground cumin

1ml paprika

45ml olive oil

30ml lemon juice (or more to taste)

125ml chopped coriander

Prepare the puri and arrange on a tray.

DUKKA Toss the hazelnuts into a large frying pan and roast for a few minutes until the skins brown and loosen. Remove from the pan and rub off the skins with your hands.

Chop the nuts roughly, then return to the frying pan with the sesame, cumin and coriander seeds. Continue cooking until everything is lightly roasted, and the kitchen smells like heaven. Remove from the heat, mix in the thyme and season with salt and pepper. Grind the dukka to a rough crumble in a grinder or with a pestle and mortar. Tip into a bowl.

BUTTER BEAN MASH Mash the beans in a bowl, then mix in the remaining ingredients. Check the consistency; if it's too stiff you might need to add a little more olive oil.

Top bits of puri with butter bean mash and sprinkle dukka on top.

chicken satay

Any type of meat may be used for satay, including beef, lamb, ostrich, venison and pork. The skewers may be assembled a couple of hours before cooking; keep covered and chilled. Peanut sauce is fine in the fridge for three days.

serves 6 to 8

4 skinless, filleted chicken
  breasts
60ml peanut or vegetable oil
Garam Masala (page 214)

PEANUT SAUCE
100g roasted and salted peanuts
6 spring onions, trimmed and chopped
1 garlic clove
1 red chilli, sliced and seeded
30ml soy sauce
finely grated zest and juice of ½ lemon
5ml brown sugar
2ml ground cumin
125ml coconut cream
60ml chopped coriander
45ml crunchy peanut butter

If you're planning to braai the satays, soak about 20 slim bamboo skewers in cold water for an hour to prevent them from scorching. Cut the chicken into slim slices and place in a dish. Pour over the oil and turn the meat to coat well. Spear onto skewers and dust with a little garam masala.

PEANUT SAUCE Grind the peanuts, spring onions, garlic and chilli to a fairly coarse paste in a food processor or with a pestle and mortar. Mix in the soy sauce, lemon zest and juice, brown sugar, cumin and coconut cream. Stir in the coriander and peanut butter, cover and chill until serving time.

For the best flavour, braai the satays briefly over hot coals. Alternatively, sizzle in a ridged pan or under the oven grill with a strip of foil shielding the skewers from the heat. Arrange on a plate with the sauce served separately for dipping.

spicy chunks of meat threaded on skewers and grilled over the coals originated in java or sumatra in indonesia and feature throughout southeast asia in countries like malaysia, singapore, thailand and the philippines.

there was a time when crayfish were plentiful and cheap. early cookbooks called them 'kreeft', which was later shortened to 'kreef'.

crayfish
IN avocado

We call this delectable seafood crayfish, even though their official title is rock lobster. In the 1960s Avocado Ritz was all the rage, with monkfish sometimes plumping out the more costly shellfish. The idea for this snazzy dish was formed a century earlier, when crayfish in a mayonnaisey sauce was piled onto lettuce with a garnish of hard-boiled egg and sliced cucumber, with lobster coral triumphantly rounding out the presentation.

serves 2

1 crayfish
1 avocado
lemon juice
salt and milled black pepper
paprika, for garnishing
lemon wedges, for squeezing

SHERRY MAYONNAISE
125ml medium cream sherry
60ml cream
125ml mayonnaise

Place the crayfish in a small saucepan with a cupful of cold water. Cover and boil for 6 to 8 minutes, depending on size. Deshell, devein and cut the tail meat into small cubes. Snap the claws and extricate the meat. Cut off the tail shell.

Cut the avocado in half; remove and discard the peel and pip. Slice slivers from the rounded sides so they stand level. Brush the cut edges with lemon juice to avoid discolouration, and season with a little salt and pepper. Place the avocado halves on serving plates.

SHERRY MAYONNAISE Pour the sherry into a small saucepan and boil uncovered until reduced to a thin syrup. Allow to cool, then mix in the cream, mayonnaise and crayfish meat. Season with salt and pepper.

Spoon the crayfish into the avocado hollows and sprinkle with a little paprika. Garnish with the tail shells and place lemon wedges on the side for squeezing.

smoked
fish sambal

Recipes for gestampte snoek (pounded snoek, not unlike a firm pâté) were brought to the Cape Colony by Malays in the seventeenth century. A similar 'fish cream' of British travellers in the 1920s and 1930s was much blander and mixed with milk to the consistency of mashed potato. Smoked snoek is preferred for its excellent flavour and firm texture, though any smoked fish will do.

serves 4 to 6

200g smoked fish
30g butter
1 onion, finely chopped
1 green chilli, seeded and finely chopped
15ml lemon juice
30ml chopped parsley
salt and milled black pepper

Skin, bone and flake the fish. Heat the butter in a frying pan and fry the onion and chilli until translucent. Remove from the heat and mix in the flaked fish, lemon juice and parsley. Season with salt and pepper. Scoop the mixture into a bowl. Serve with crusty bread.

ROASTED PUMPKIN SOUP

American Indians supped enthusiastically on pumpkins from the earliest times. Conquering Spaniards took one bite, loved the stuff, and took seeds back to Europe, where cultivation commenced, later spreading to the Middle East. Closer to home, pumpkin was one of the first crops to grow successfully in the Cape of Good Hope. History doesn't record whether gardeners got the idea from Holland or from resident black clans, who had been feasting on pumpkin for a couple of hundred years.

serves 8

1kg pumpkin
olive oil
15ml brown sugar
salt and milled black pepper
2 onions, chopped
1,2 litres hot Chicken Stock (page 216)
1ml grated nutmeg
roasted pumpkin pips, for garnishing

Heat the oven to 220°C. Skin and pip the pumpkin and cut into cubes. Lay in a roaster, sprinkle with olive oil and season with brown sugar and a little salt and pepper. Roast uncovered for about 20 minutes until golden.

Lightly brown the onions in olive oil in a large saucepan. Add the roasted pumpkin, stock and nutmeg. Cover and simmer for about 20 minutes until the pumpkin is soft.

Purée the soup. Before serving, reheat, check the flavour and adjust if necessary. Scatter roasted pumpkin pips on each bowl before serving.

BUTTERNUT MAY BE USED INSTEAD OF PUMPKIN IN THIS SIMPLE SOUP, AND A DASH OF CURRY POWDER IS A DELICIOUS VARIATION ON THIS PLAINER THEME. AND, FOR AN EVEN RICHER BROTH, STIR IN A LITTLE CREAM AT THE END OF THE COOKING TIME.

BOONTJIESOP

This comfort-zone recipe has its roots in Germany and calls for patience, as the ingredients need to simmer long and slow for their flavours and textures to meld. It's even better next day, when the beans have spent time in the flavoursome broth. Use any type of dried beans that take your fancy. They do require pre-soaking though, either overnight in plenty of cold water or the quicker way described below.

serves 8

500g beef shin (on the bone)
250g dried beans
vegetable oil
100g chopped, smoked pork lardons or rindless bacon
1 onion, finely chopped
1,5 litres hot Beef Stock (page 217)
2 bay leaves
1 turnip, peeled and finely chopped
1 carrot, peeled and finely chopped
4 ripe tomatoes, blanched, skinned and finely chopped, or
    400g tin whole peeled tomatoes, chopped in their juice
salt and milled black pepper

Trim the meat of excess fat. To pre-soak the beans, rinse well then tip into a medium saucepan and cover generously with cold water. Bring to the boil, then simmer for 5 minutes. Remove from the heat and set aside for an hour. Drain.

Heat a little oil in a large saucepan and fry the lardons or bacon until the fat has rendered. Stir in the onion and fry until translucent. Add the stock, beans, beef shin and bay leaves, gently crushed to release their flavour. Cover and simmer for 1½ to 2 hours until the beans are very tender. Don't be in a rush; the cooking time will depend on the type and age of the beans.

Add the turnip, carrots and tomatoes and season the soup with salt and pepper. Cover and simmer for about 30 minutes more until the vegetables are cooked. Check and adjust the flavour if necessary.

CURRIED fish SOUP

Seafood soups often included handfuls of freshly-gathered seaweed for extra nourishment. The best fish soup is prepared with several types of fish. To make it ahead of time, prepare the soup prior to adding the fish. Chill for up to a day, then reheat, add the fish and complete the recipe.

serves 8 to 10

2–3 smallish fish (about 3kg in total), filleted
    (retain heads and bones)
butter and vegetable oil
2 onions, finely sliced
2 carrots, peeled and finely sliced
2 celery sticks, finely chopped
2 garlic cloves, finely chopped
small knob ginger, peeled and grated
10ml curry powder
2ml turmeric
4 ripe tomatoes, blanched, skinned and
    chopped, or 400g tin whole peeled
    tomatoes, chopped in their juice
1,5 litres hot Fish Stock (page 216), or water
4 potatoes, peeled and cut into cubes
salt and milled black pepper

Rinse the fish heads and bones. Skin the meat and cut into chunks. Heat a generous amount of butter and oil in a large saucepan and fry the onions, carrots, celery, garlic and ginger until softened. Stir in the curry powder and turmeric.

Add the tomatoes, stock or water and fish heads and bones. Cover and simmer for about 20 minutes.

Remove and discard the fish bones and heads. Add the potatoes to the soup and season with salt and pepper. Cover and simmer for about 10 minutes until the potato is soft.

Add the fish, cover and simmer for about 5 minutes until cooked. Check and adjust the flavour if necessary.

fisherfolk never allow anything to go to waste. in this time-honoured west coast dish flavours are faithful to cape malay cooks, who count curried snoek head soup among their favourites.

black mussel soup

From the earliest times, limpets, perlemoen and black and white mussels were collected by coast-dwellers and made into soup. Limpets and perlemoen require long, gentle cooking, but black mussels are done in a trice. Older recipes called for the meat to be minced, pounded or chopped. They're much more toothsome on the shell.

serves 6 to 8

36 black mussels, well scrubbed
500ml water
50g butter
1 onion, finely chopped
45ml cake flour
125ml dry white wine
30ml chopped parsley
1 bay leaf or lemon leaf, lightly crushed
1ml grated nutmeg
milled black pepper
125ml cream

Carefully pull out the mussel beards and place the mussels in a saucepan with the water. Cover and boil until they open; this should only take 5 or 6 minutes. Discard any that remain shut. Lift the mussels from the pan and set aside. Strain the mussel liquor.

Heat the butter in a clean saucepan and fry the onion until translucent. Remove from the heat and blend in the flour, then stir in the wine and mussel liquor. Stir over medium heat until the soup thickens. Add the parsley and bay or lemon leaf, and season with nutmeg and a little pepper. Add salt only if necessary; mussel liquor is naturally salty. Cover and simmer very gently for 10 minutes.

Just before serving, add the cream and mussels and heat through.

spiced tomato soup

Tomatoes need to be at the peak of perfection – full of sweet flavour – so purchase them ahead of time and let them ripen in a warm spot if necessary. Tinned tomatoes should be used only as a last resort. Optional garnishes include crusty bread or crisp croûtons.

serves 6 to 8

800g very ripe tomatoes, or 800g tin
   whole peeled tomatoes, chopped
   in their juice
30g butter
1 onion, finely chopped
1 litre hot vegetable stock
2ml Green Masala (page 213),
   or 1 green chilli, seeded and
   finely chopped
5ml paprika
5ml sugar
1 cinnamon stick
4 whole cloves
1 bay leaf, lightly crushed
salt and milled black pepper

Blanch, skin and roughly chop the tomatoes. Melt the butter in a large saucepan and fry the onion long and slow until richly coloured and jammy. This will bring out the natural sweetness, which is vital for the flavour of the soup.

Add the tomatoes, stock, masala or chilli, paprika, sugar, cinnamon, cloves and bay leaf, and season with salt and pepper.

Cover and simmer for about 20 minutes. Serve hot or chilled.

there's an Indian bias to this zesty soup, though you're welcome to leave out the masala or chilli if you can't take the heat.

chicken soup

This is a free adaptation of many variations of this creamy African soup that is popular throughout the continent. Early recipes specified mace and nutmeg as the only flavourings, and called for egg yolks to be added at the end, resulting in an even richer broth. Optional garnishes include coriander leaves or sprigs of watercress, which grew wild in water furrows at the Cape, and were used with various wild lettuces in early salads. Plain or spiced rice was often served as an accompaniment to soup. Here rice is in the broth, adding texture and richness. A handful of crushed, roasted peanuts is another African-style idea.

serves 8 to 10

1 small chicken (about 1kg)
2 litres hot Chicken Stock (page 216)
1 onion, chopped
2 carrots, peeled and sliced
1 celery stick, sliced (leaves and stem)
small bunch fresh herbs (parsley, bay leaf, fennel)
4 cardamom pods, lightly crushed
2ml turmeric
salt and milled black pepper
60ml uncooked long-grain rice
250ml cream or coconut cream

Wash the chicken and place in a large saucepan. Pour in the stock, then add the onion, carrots, celery, herbs, cardamom and turmeric. Season with salt and pepper. Cover and simmer for about 50 minutes until the chicken is cooked.

Discard the herbs. Lift the chicken from the pan and cool a little. Remove and discard the skin and bones and roughly shred the meat.

Strain the stock into a clean saucepan, add the rice, cover and simmer for about 30 minutes until very soft and almost melting into the broth. Add the cream or coconut cream and chicken meat and heat through. Check the flavour and adjust if necessary.

mulligatawny soup

This recipe was introduced to South Africa by early British food writers like Mrs HM Slade and S van H Tulleken. They, in turn, learned it from the British Raj, who spent years in India as army officers, civil servants and diplomats. Authenticate the presentation by offering a bowl of plain or spiced rice as an accompaniment.

serves 8 to 10

1 small chicken (about 1kg)	15ml curry powder
2,5 litres hot Beef Stock (page 217)	1 carrot, peeled and chopped
vegetable oil	1 turnip, peeled and chopped
2 onions, finely chopped	2 granny smith apples, peeled,
4 garlic cloves, finely chopped	cored and chopped
1 green chilli, sliced and seeded	2 celery sticks, sliced
60ml chopped parsley	salt and milled black pepper
30ml chopped mint	10ml tamarind pulp
30ml chopped thyme	30ml rice flour
2ml ground mace	125ml semi-sweet white wine

Wash the chicken and place in a large saucepan. Pour in the stock, cover and simmer for about 50 minutes until cooked. Lift the bird from the stock. When it's cool enough to handle, remove the skin and bones and roughly shred the meat. Reserve the stock.

Heat a little oil in a large saucepan and fry the onions until translucent. Stir in the garlic, chilli, parsley, mint, thyme, mace and curry powder. Add the carrot, turnip, apples, celery and stock. Season with salt and pepper. Cover and simmer for about 15 minutes until the vegetables are tender. Add the shredded chicken to the soup.

Mix the tamarind and rice flour into a cupful of the hot broth. Add to the soup with the wine, and stir until it thickens. Check the flavour and adjust if necessary.

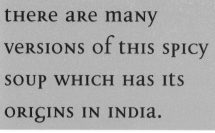

there are many versions of this spicy soup which has its origins in india.

wild flowers & waterblommetjies; shipwrecks & seafood

west coast & namaqualand

5

THE SUN-SPLASHED WEST COAST AND NAMAQUALAND IS BIG SKY COUNTRY, A PLACE OF CONTRASTS, CONTRADICTIONS AND TIMELESS BEAUTY. SEEDS OF OUR MULTI-CULTURAL HISTORY WERE SOWN HERE, AND LOCALS LEARNED TO TRIUMPH OVER A HARSH CLIMATE AND AN UNCOMPROMISING ENVIRONMENT.

Portuguese seafarers encountered Africa's earliest inhabitants along the coast, 'swarthy men who eat sea wolves and whales, the flesh of gazelles, and the roots of plants and honey'. The sailors were tracking ancient legends about a mystical world deep in the southern Atlantic, voyages of discovery spurred on by trade and the establishment of a sea route to the Indies.

The West Coast is the ultimate bolt hole for those stressed out by city living. It is vast, flat, silent and seemingly barren; from one horizon to the other little disturbs the line of vision. Stay awhile. Stroll along a beach and feel the sand between your toes. Wander through the wilds and discover a world of tortoises and tumbleweeds, shipwrecks and seafood.

There are no pretensions of grandeur except for a breathtaking natural marvel each spring: after winter rains have soaked the veld, wild flowers bloom in an almost indecent array of glory, too quickly to fade into the oblivion of the monochromatic landscape. The unique fynbos, part of the Cape Floral Kingdom, is the largest remaining tract of natural vegetation of its type in the world.

The land is locked between the icy Atlantic Ocean and the rugged mountains of the Bokkeveld and Cederberg, stretching north to the desert's doorstep and the Great Karoo. Areas are known by time-honoured names like Swartland, Strandveld, Hantam, Knersvlakte,

Voor-Boesmanland, Hardeveld, Richtersveld and Sandveld, a narrow coastal strip forming a natural buffer between sea and inland regions.

For thousands of years this was home to the San (Bushmen), Khoikhoi (Hottentots), Strandlopers (also called Watermen, outcasts from the Khoikhoi community), and Nama – from whom Namaqualand was named. Historians named these genetically-similar people Khoisan, hunter-gatherers who bagged wild game and scratched a meagre existence from seashore and scrub. They brewed liquor from roots, infused fruits for beverages and plucked berries and seeds for snacks.

Wild figs are eaten fresh and made into jam; Cape sorrel is simmered into soup and added to stews; pelargonium petals are used as a herb; various spinach-type plants, like hotnotskool (Hottentots' cabbage, 'better than asparagus') and kinkelbossie (twisted bush) are added to bredies.

Seafood, nourished by the icy Benguela current that sweeps the coast, has always sustained the locals. Proof of this was found in the middens of Strandlopers who left piles of fish bones and shells. Their catch was either eaten immediately (perhaps grilled over open coals) or preserved by drying and salting. Weathered folk still pit their skills against nature to catch anchovies, snoek, galjoen, hottentot, silverfish, white stumpnose, elf, harders, kabeljou, geelbek and crayfish.

TOP LEFT: *A net-full of freshly-caught crayfish ready for cooking in a pot of water or over the coals of a braai.*

TOP CENTRE: *A fishing boat on the sands of the Langebaan lagoon.*

TOP RIGHT: *Signboards at the general dealer store in the quaint fishing village of Paternoster.*

ABOVE: *Holiday homes and fishermen's cottages rim the beach at Paternoster.*

TOP LEFT: *Old farmhouse at Niewoudville in Namaqualand.*

CENTRE LEFT: *Fresh waterblommetjies.*

LEFT: *Bokkoms hang in bunches ready for snacking.*

ABOVE: *Majestic kokerbome grow tall in the desert landscape of Namaqualand.*

RIGHT: *Sunrise over Langebaan lagoon from the stoep of a cottage.*

Harbours dotting the coastline provide safe havens for boats, and factories to process their catch – filleting, freezing, smoking, drying, canning, grinding into fish meal and rendering it into oil. Lambert's Bay, focus of the crayfish industry, has one of the prettiest harbours of all which forms a bridge to Bird Island, breeding place of the Cape Gannet and Cormorant, just two of the many types of birds that call the West Coast home. Further south is Saldanha Bay, where mussels and oysters are farmed.

Casual open-air restaurants are a feature of coastal towns. Seafood bisque is ladled from huge pots. Snoek are sploshed with garlicky butter as they sizzle over open coals. Hot-smoked linefish emerges from smokers. Huge loaves of bread are baked in traditional bakoonde (ovens) and spread with farm butter and konfyt (jam). Trays are piled with black mussels and crayfish. Bredies are served in potjies – the same fat-bellied three-legged pots that accompanied old-timers on their treks through the country. Ingredients patiently simmer away to that inevitable stage where meat and sauce merge into a delicious union, vegetables unashamedly mushy, never crisp-tender in today's designer mode.

Protein-rich bokkems (from the Dutch 'bokking', meaning herring) are a popular local snack. Small fish like harders are salted, tied into bunches and dried. Fishermen rely on them to predict a change in the weather; when they drip, rain will fall. The practical explanation has more to do with reason than folklore – the high salt content of the fish combines with the increased humidity of the air to produce the effect.

If dried fish isn't your idea of heaven, you may prefer other local delights like peertjies (spiced lamb's testicles), pofadders (lamb's intestines filled with offal and cooked over the coals), or skilpadjies (caul fat wrapped around liver). Happily, tortoises – from which skilpadjies get their name – are no longer turned into soup. Now protected, they are free to roam in peace, and road signs request motorists carry them to the safety of the fynbos.

Twigs and leaves of the rooibos (red bush), which grows along the Olifants River and high in the Cederberg, are dried and made into tea; it is farmed nowhere else in the world. Today it is the preferred beverage, not only of locals (who claim to be the best rooibos-brewers in the land), but health-conscious folk all over the world.

Waterblommetjies (little water flowers) bloom in vleis, dams and streams. This unique vegetable has been informally harvested for centuries; now farmers grow plants in specially prepared ponds. There are other indigenous foods to enjoy, like uintjies (peel, boil and enjoy their chestnut-peanut flavour) and heerbone (the Lord's beans) which pad out bredies and curries. Sandveld sugar pumpkins, with skin the colour of rich Kalahari soil and flesh of yellow, make 'the best fritters in the world'.

Throughout most of the region soil is too poor to sustain agriculture to any great extent, except in the lush Olifants River Valley where groves of citrus grow, and the Swartland – named after the dark soil and scrub-like vegetation – which is the hub of a rich wheat industry and heart of the wine route that sprawls from Malmesbury in the south to Mamre, Riebeek-Kasteel, Riebeek West, Porterville, Piketberg and Citrusdal.

The Khoisan are long gone; elephants and antelope no longer run wild and free and, thanks to plundering whalers, these gentle giants of the deep are few and far between. Highways and byways are relatively free of hordes of tourists, unspoilt beaches are uncrowded and unlittered, and life slips by much the way it has done for many, many years.

West Coast doors are open to friends who pop in for a chat and a cup of tea or a drink or two of something stronger. Guest houses offer country-style hospitality in keeping with the laid-back mood, and restaurants specialize in the freshest seafood to be found anywhere in the country, plainly cooked and designed to fill tummies rather than tease tastebuds in the mode of city cuisine.

When your pace has slowed to the West Coast beat and you take your leave of this placid land, it will be with the hope that not much will change before you return for another glimpse of the simple life, and a host of homely dishes that are faithful to recipes of days gone by.

GROWING YOUR OWN VEGETABLES IN A PATCH OF SOIL CLOSE TO HOME IS A PRACTICAL AND SOUL-SOOTHING SOLUTION TO FEEDING THE FAMILY.

salads, vegetables & grains

THE HIGH COST of meat means that alternative sources of nutrition play a starring role in the African diet. It also means that cooks through the ages have become extremely inventive in their ways of preparing vegetables, pulses and grains.

A variety of greens have grown wild since the mists of time. The San (Bushmen), wandering pastoralists and trek-farmers gathered it from the veld, learning which bulbs, shoots, roots, seeds, flowers and leaves were nutritious.

Later, crops like maize, millet, melons, beans, gourds, sugar cane and grain sorghum (used as a grain as well as to brew beer) were cultivated. Way back in the eleventh century, melon pips and sorghum seeds were discovered near the Limpopo River, proof that agriculture has been practised for many centuries.

Best-known veld food is morogo or imfino which is, in fact, the leaves of more than a hundred different varieties of plants, each distinctly flavoured. The leaves, pods and tendrils are carefully plucked so as not to damage the plant. Morogo is cooked solo as a vegetable, and served with meat or pap (maize meal). Although morogo is most often very simply prepared, modern additions include onions, tomatoes, peanuts, potatoes and chilli. Spinach and kale are good substitutes for morogo.

Protein-rich legumes have long been grown in rural gardens and on farms, specifically jugo beans, mung beans and cowpeas which, despite its name, is a bean. Groundnuts (peanuts) from northern parts of the continent and pumpkin (from America) are more recent additions to the African table.

Young fruit and leaves of hard-skinned gourds are delicious, while pods are used as calabashes, eating vessels and household containers. They are dried or baked to strengthen the skin, then cut open and cleaned out. Pebbles, sand or seeds are swirled around to polish the inner surfaces.

Immigrants to Africa added their own inimitable stamp to the art of vegetable cooking, especially after the Dutch planted their famous vegetable gardens at the Cape from seeds they brought from Europe. Recipes followed the seventeenth century European style: droogkoek (dry-cooking – shallow frying in butter or fat), boiling and mashing, and creaming (simmering in cream). Most popular was glazing – vegetables stewed in bouillon with lavish quantities of butter and sugar.

Lowveld salad

Early salads included a variety of wild lettuces, watercress (which grew along the waterways of the Cape Peninsula and Boland) and soft, young shoots of the palmiet bulrush. Roots, stems and leaves of sorrel added a sourish tang. I discovered this salad many years ago at a game lodge on the banks of the Makhutswi River in the Mpumalanga Lowveld.

serves 6

mixed salad leaves

1 avocado

½ pawpaw

1 red onion, finely sliced

50g macadamia nuts

MUSTARD SEED DRESSING

125ml vegetable or olive oil

30ml lemon juice

30ml white wine vinegar

5ml dijon mustard

10ml wholegrain mustard

5ml honey

salt and milled black pepper

Arrange the salad leaves on a platter. Peel, pip and slice the avocado and pawpaw. Arrange on the leaves and top with onion. Roughly chop the macadamias and roast in a dry frying pan.

MUSTARD SEED DRESSING Mix the ingredients together until well blended.

Pour the dressing over the salad and scatter over the nuts.

kachoomer

This simple Indian salad of tomato and onion is glossed with a glorious cumin-based dressing. For the best flavour, ensure that your tomatoes are at the peak of ripe perfection.

serves 4

1 red onion, finely sliced

2–3 tomatoes

10ml cumin seeds

2ml salt

5ml sugar

60ml white or red wine vinegar

juice of ½ lemon

30ml vegetable oil

coriander leaves, for garnishing

Pour boiling water over the onion, set aside for about 5 minutes, then drain well. Slice the tomatoes into wedges and arrange on a plate with the onion.

Roast the cumin seeds lightly in a dry frying pan. Grind fairly finely with the salt and sugar with a pestle and mortar. Mix in the vinegar, lemon juice and oil.

Pour the dressing over the salad and garnish with coriander.

if possible, source
luscious vine-ripened
tomatoes for this
flavoursome salad.

stampkoring with onion and tomato

Stampkoring – pearled wheat or wheat rice – is a healthy, nutty flavoured alternative to rice. It's easy to flossy-up into interesting, no-fuss vegetarian dishes like this one.

serves 6

200g stampkoring (pearled wheat)

750ml Chicken Stock (page 216)

2ml salt

2ml turmeric

vegetable oil

2 onions, sliced

12 small tomatoes, cut into halves
   or quarters (depending on size)

30ml chopped parsley

30ml chopped mint

Rinse the stampkoring with cold water, then tip into a medium saucepan. Add the stock, salt and turmeric, cover and simmer for 20 to 30 minutes under tender. Drain well in a colander.

Heat a little oil in a frying pan and lightly brown the onions. Stir in the stampkoring, tomatoes, parsley and mint, and heat through. Tip into a serving dish and serve hot or cool.

carrot salad

Prior to landing on the dinner table, carrots were classed as weeds and used as cattle feed. They originated in Afghanistan early in the seventh century. The Moors brought the seeds along the coast of North Africa to Western Europe, from where carrots spread to Spain, France, England and Holland, and eventually, the southern tip of Africa. This tangy carrot salad comes from the farming heartland of South Africa, the Free State, formerly known as the Orange Free State.

serves 4 to 6

500g carrots

1 onion, finely sliced

125ml water

125ml red wine vinegar

60ml vegetable oil

80g sugar

5ml mustard seeds

1ml prepared English mustard

salt and milled black pepper

Peel the carrots and cut into slim batons. Cook in a saucepan of salted boiling water until fairly tender. Drain, then tip into a bowl.

Combine the remaining ingredients in a medium saucepan and bring to the boil, stirring until the sugar dissolves. Simmer for about 5 minutes until the onion is soft. Pour the hot sauce over the carrots and set aside for an hour or two to marinate. Serve cool.

slaphakskeentjies

Tiny onions in a creamy, sweetish-sour sauce is a famous Cape Dutch dish that may be served hot or cool. It's best to make the sauce just before serving.

serves 6

750g pickling onions
3 eggs
30ml sugar
5ml dry English mustard
2ml salt
125ml white wine or cider vinegar
30ml water
200ml cream

Peel the onions and cook in a saucepan of salted boiling water until just tender but not overcooked. Drain and tip into a serving bowl.

Combine the eggs, sugar, mustard and salt in a medium saucepan off the heat. Whisk with a hand whisk until frothy. Stir in the vinegar, water and cream, then place over low heat and cook, stirring constantly, until the sauce thickens.

Pour over the onions and serve at once, or allow to cool and offer at room temperature.

these dishes are good examples of simple, comforting recipes that are perfect in a homely setting.

pap with spinach

Mixing wild greens (morogo or imfino) with pap (maize meal) is popular in tribal villages within easy reach of places where wild greens grow. This recipe brings that idea right up to date.

serves 8 to 10

1 bunch spinach
750ml vegetable stock
1ml turmeric
2ml salt
100g maize meal
125ml cream (approximate amount)

Wash the spinach in plenty of cold water, then trim the thick stalks and roughly shred the leaves.

Bring the stock to the boil in a medium saucepan. Add the turmeric and salt, then stir in the maize meal. Cover and simmer over very low heat for 10 minutes until the maize meal is cooked. Stir occasionally.

Stir in the spinach and cream, cover and set aside for about an hour to thicken. Shortly before serving, reheat and check the consistency; the pap may have firmed up and you may need to add a little more cream.

umngqusho with sweetcorn

Two indigenous varieties of beans – jugo beans and cowpeas – were used for umngqusho in the past; any dried beans may be substituted. Samp is dried maize which is stamped and coarsely ground.

serves 6

100g samp
100g dried beans
1,2 litres water, plus extra for soaking
salt and milled black pepper
400g tin whole kernel corn, drained

Rinse the samp and beans with cold water, then tip into a bowl and add cold water to cover generously. Cover and set aside for about 8 hours to soak. Alternatively – if you're pressed for time – place in a medium saucepan, add cold water to cover, bring to the boil and cook for 5 minutes. Remove from the heat and allow to soak for an hour. Drain.

Bring 1,2 litres water to the boil in a medium saucepan. Add the samp and beans, cover and cook over very low heat for about 1½ hours until very tender. The cooking time depends on the type of bean as well as the age (the older the tougher). Start checking for doneness after an hour.

Drain the samp and beans. Season with salt and pepper. Add the sweetcorn and heat through. Drain, tip into a warm bowl, and serve hot.

To make this dish into a salad, toss with Mustard Seed Dressing (page 58) and serve cool.

glazed carrots

My grandmother mashed carrots and potatoes with butter, milk and a touch of mace or nutmeg. For posher occasions, she added egg yolks and folded in whipped egg white to make a light soufflé. Sweet glazed carrots are even more popular, especially with roast meat.

serves 8

2 bunches young carrots
125ml water
150g butter, cut into cubes
45ml honey or brown
   sugar
2ml grated nutmeg
2 star anise

Peel the carrots and slice into slim batons. Heat the water in a wide saucepan, add the carrots, butter, honey or sugar, nutmeg and star anise. Cover and cook very gently for 5 to 8 minutes until the carrots are almost done (the cooking time will depend on how they've been cut).

Uncover, increase the heat and continue cooking until the sauce has reduced to a glaze. Toss the carrots about in the pan from time to time so they glaze evenly. Tip into a warm serving dish and serve hot.

UMNGQUSHO — also called GNUSH — is a simple dish of samp and beans. it's a staple in black communities and served at celebrations from harvest festivals to wedding feasts.

everybody
adores rice,
a menu
cornerstone
of many
sectors of
our multi-
cultural
community.

yellow rice

Rice was one crop that failed at the Cape, so huge quantities have to be imported. The addition or turmeric (called borrie here) was introduced by Indian immigrants who worked on the sugar plantations in Natal (now KwaZulu-Natal). Another name for this dish is begrafnisrys (funeral rice), as it's always part of the meal served after funerals.

serves 4

200g uncooked long-grain rice
50g seedless raisins
4 whole cloves
5ml salt
1ml turmeric
625ml water
30g butter

Combine the rice, raisins, cloves, salt, turmeric and water in a medium saucepan. Cover and bring to the boil, then reduce the heat and simmer for about 20 minutes until the rice is cooked and the water has been absorbed.

Add the butter and fluff the rice up with a fork. Transfer to a warm bowl and serve hot.

spicy rice with peas

Gesmoorde ertjie rys (braised pea rice) is a gently-flavoured Cape Malay rice dish that is a glorious foil to highly-spiced dishes like breyanis and curries.

serves 6

butter and vegetable oil
1 onion, finely chopped
5ml cumin seeds
3 cardamom pods, lightly crushed
1 cassia or cinnamon stick
2ml turmeric
2ml ground allspice
3 whole cloves
200g uncooked long-grain rice
5ml salt
500ml water
200g frozen peas, defrosted

Heat a little butter and oil in a medium saucepan and fry the onion until golden. Add the cumin, cardamom, cassia or cinnamon, turmeric, allspice and cloves, and sizzle for about 15 seconds until the spices are aromatic.

Stir in the rice, then add the salt and water. Cover and simmer for about 20 minutes until the rice is cooked and the water has been absorbed. Stir in the peas a few minutes before the end of the cooking time. Tip into a warm bowl and serve hot.

roasted beetroot and onion

An earlier version of this Afrikaner salad called for sliced beetroot and onion; roasting the vegetables results in a far more rustic and flavoursome mélange. According to early food writers, the best beetroot should be 'no larger than the size of a bantam's egg', so these are the ones to seek out. Choose a bunch of even-sized beets so they roast evenly.

serves 4 to 6

4–6 medium beetroot, washed
1 onion, sliced into wedges
4 bay leaves, lightly crushed
olive oil
salt and milled black pepper
125ml red wine vinegar
60ml water
30ml brown sugar

Heat the oven to 200°C. Cut off the beetroot leaves at the stem. Depending on size, cut the beetroot into halves or quarters (leave the skin on) and toss into a roaster with the onion. Tuck the bay leaves in here and there. Drizzle with olive oil and season with salt and pepper. Cover with foil and bake for 45 minutes. Remove the foil and toss the vegetables about in the pan juices. Increase the heat to 220°C and roast for about 15 minutes more until lightly charred. Lift the vegetables into a serving dish.

Add the vinegar, water and brown sugar to the pan juices, and season with salt and pepper. Bring to the boil, stirring until the sugar dissolves. Boil uncovered until the sauce thickens slightly. Pour over the beetroot and allow to cool.

this is an example of taking a historical, classic recipe and making it fresher and more contemporary.

spinach with tomatoes and peanuts

A variety of wild, nutritious greens are gathered by rural blacks from the open veld and near streams. The Nguni call it imfino; the Sotho name is morogo or moroho. It's sorted, washed and simply cooked as a vegetable or served with meat and pap (maize meal). Spinach is a good substitute for the wild greens; adding tomatoes and peanuts gives the dish a modern spin.

serves 6

400g spinach
vegetable oil
1 onion, thickly sliced
500g small roma tomatoes
salt and milled black pepper
50g roasted and salted peanuts

Wash the spinach in plenty of cold water, then trim the thick stalks and roughly shred the leaves.

Heat a little oil in a large frying pan and fry the onion until golden. Add the tomatoes and spinach, and season with salt and pepper. Stir everything together. Cook briskly until the spinach is limp.

Tip the vegetables into a bowl, scatter the peanuts on top and serve hot.

CINNAMON-ROASTED PUMPKIN

Rural folk cook pumpkin simply – sliced and boiled, or cooked with maize kernels, pap (maize meal) or beans. Early Dutch cooks mashed pumpkin with butter, sugar and cinnamon; this is an adaptation of that idea. The oven heat and cooking time aren't crucial, as pumpkin is normally roasted at the same time as meat. Butternut can be used instead of pumpkin if you wish and leftovers whip up deliciously into Pumpkin Fritters (page 175).

PUMPKINS WERE GROWN IN AFRICA LONG BEFORE THE CAPE WAS COLONIZED, AND ITS POPULARITY ENDURES TO THIS DAY.

serves 6

750g pumpkin
125ml orange juice or water
salt
2 cinnamon sticks
50g brown sugar
100g butter, cut into cubes

Heat the oven to 180°C. Peel the pumpkin, cut into slices and remove the pips.

Arrange the pumpkin in a baking dish. Add the orange juice or water and salt lightly. Crumble in the cinnamon, sprinkle with sugar and dot with butter. Cover with the lid or foil.

Bake for 30 minutes, then uncover and baste the pumpkin with the sauce. Roast uncovered for a further 30 to 45 minutes until tender and well browned – switch on the oven griller at the end of cooking time if it needs more colour.

Transfer to a serving dish and serve hot.

vegetable and dhal curry

Meat is a luxury in many homes and housewives are adept at creating wonderful stand-alone vegetarian dishes using dhal (lentils) and vegetables. Here's a flavoursome Cape Malay curry with a strong Indian influence. You don't have to stay with the vegetables listed; choose your favourites. And if you don't have roasted masala at hand, use curry powder instead.

serves 4 to 6

500g vegetables (cauliflower, carrots, green beans)
150g brown lentils
vegetable oil
1 onion, finely chopped
4 garlic cloves, crushed
1 green chilli, finely sliced and seeded
1 cinnamon stick
3 cardamom pods, lightly crushed
5ml Roasted Masala (page 213), or curry powder
5ml ground cumin
5ml ground coriander
2ml turmeric
salt and milled black pepper
2 very ripe tomatoes, finely chopped
500ml water

Prepare the vegetables: cut the cauliflower into florets; slice the carrots into batons; cut the beans in half.

Rinse the lentils, then tip into a small saucepan with cold water to cover generously. Cover and simmer for 15 minutes. Drain.

Heat a little oil in a large saucepan and fry the onion until golden. Stir in the garlic, chilli, cinnamon, cardamom, masala or curry powder, cumin, coriander and turmeric, and sizzle for about 15 seconds. Season with salt and pepper. Stir in the tomatoes, lentils and water, cover and simmer for about 30 minutes until the lentils are almost tender.

Mix in the vegetables with a little more salt and pepper, cover and simmer for about 20 minutes until tender. If the curry is too moist, cook uncovered for a few minutes. Serve hot with sambals if you wish.

orchards & oysters;
farmlands & frontiers

the overberg, garden route & eastern cape

7

THE LUSH CAPE WINELANDS GIVE WAY TO THE SUN-DAPPLED OVERBERG AND SOUTHERN COASTAL AREAS. TRAVEL ON TO ENJOY THE PLEASURES OF THE WORLD-FAMOUS (AND APTLY-NAMED) GARDEN ROUTE, THEN EXPLORE THE HISTORIC EASTERN CAPE 'SETTLER COUNTRY'.

The route of white expansion from the fledgling Cape Colony during the late seventeenth century established new farmlands and forged new frontiers. Adventurers travelled through splendid coastal scenery, encountered wild animals and, on the far eastern border with Transkei, came into conflict with blacks journeying south. Their mission was similar: to find a settled place of their own. Boer trek-farmers were fleeing British dominance; black tribesmen were escaping Shaka's uprising in Zululand.

Boere bartered for sheep from resident Hottentots, and established stockposts and farms. The Overberg flourished, ultimately absorbing the Hottentots into farm life. Their successors live on in settled towns with names in a long-forgotten language – Kinko, Dipka, Napkei and Kadie – and Christian mission stations at Genadendal and Elim.

The early Overberg encompassed the area beyond the 'mountains of Africa', including Hangklip 'tot waar de macht der Hoog Edele Compagnie eindigt' – a way of saying in high Dutch that no-one could be certain where the region ended. As new districts came into being, the concept of 'over the mountain' faded. Today the Overberg refers to the region between the Riviersondered and Langeberg mountain ranges, and the sea – areas rich in natural resources and places of cultural and historical interest.

Swellendam, for example – South Africa's third oldest town – had an outspan at the Drostdy where horses were rested and travellers purchased chickens, fresh vegetables and fruit, and 'wheaten bread'. A museum has been created on the site. Flour is still ground here, the machinery powered by an ancient watermill, as it was in the eighteenth century. In valleys behind the town grow boysenberries and youngberries. Much of the crop is canned for export and turned into juice and jam, but lots of lovely, ripe berries find their way into farmstalls and onto menus of restaurants in the area.

As in past times, Overberg farmers holiday in quaint seaside towns such as Gansbaai, Onrus, Struisbaai, Cape Infanta, Waenhuiskrans (Arniston), Agulhas – the southernmost tip of the African continent – and Hermanus on Walker Bay. This is the heart of the whale route, which attracts visitors from all over the world between May and November to watch giants of the deep mate, calve and rear their young.

Linking the Overberg to the Eastern Cape is the Garden Route, 'Eden of the Cape', a melding of lush forests, ribbons of lakes, peaceful rivers, sandy beaches, placid farmlands, mighty mountain ranges and the Indian Ocean. Friendly towns tempt you to linger awhile, and local menus include regional specialities like Knysna oysters, plump East Coast soles and squid (calamari).

top Left: *Quaint fisherman's cottage at Waenhuiskrans, also known locally as Arniston.*
top centre: *Fishing boat on the slipway at Arniston.*
above: *The seaside town of Wilderness has one of the most famous beaches in the country.*

ABOVE LEFT: *The imposing Knysna Heads at the entrance to the lagoon are guarded by steep cliffs which sweep down to the sea.*

ABOVE: *Lighthouse at Cape Agulhas, the most southerly tip of Africa where the Atlantic and Indian oceans meet.*

LEFT: *A hopeful fisherman tries his luck in a peaceful lagoon.*

OPPOSITE: *A rope bridge crossing a gorge in the forest near Knysna.*

Knysna, heart of the Garden Route – named from the Khoikhoi word meaning 'straight down' (an accurate description of the sheer cliffs of the Heads that protect the lagoon from the open sea) – straddles a natural lagoon where some 200 species of fish have been recorded, including the strange, rare Knysna sea-horse. Also sheltered in the calm waters are Knysna oysters, the Garden Route's acclaimed gourmet delicacy. Oysters have been raised for 2000 years, and grow wild in many parts of the country, including Algoa Bay further north, at Cape Infanta, the mouth of the Breede River to the south, as well as on the West Coast and KwaZulu-Natal.

Despite the charms of the Garden Route, it is not in the nature of pioneers to settle. Frontiers everywhere conjure up images of confrontation, and history loves to record tales of bravery, hardship and man's triumph over adversity. The Eastern Cape typifies the vision, starting from a flashpoint of conflict, through many turbulent years, to a conclusion of a settled society.

Border clashes between trek-farmers and Xhosas resulted in many boers fleeing north. Britain brought out 1000 men and 300 women to protect the frontier. The 1820 Settlers, as they're known, were allocated farms, but knew little about agriculture. To make matters worse, the land was unsuitable for farming – it was called Zuurveld (sour land), and with good cause. Wheat crops failed, and Xhosa raids continued, forcing many new settlers to move to villages and ultimately to scatter throughout the country.

Some stayed, however, spurred on by initial agricultural failures to move in new directions. Merino sheep were imported to replace the fat-tailed sheep which had been farmed here for a very long time. Merinos, however, preferred the dry Karoo, and the sheep and wool industry shifted there and flourished. Bathurst, a minuscule town, became the heart of a thriving pineapple industry. Although much of the crop is canned for export, plenty of pineapples may be purchased at farmstalls and from hawkers in the area.

Besides being rich in natural resources, there are many picturesque Eastern Cape towns with cultural and historical roots. Grahamstown, founded in 1812 as a military outpost, is the best preserved Victorian city in the country. Cities like East London and Port Elizabeth, gateway for the 1820 Settlers, form business and holiday bases.

Many once tumbledown Eastern Cape settler homes have been renovated and preserved, some delightfully transformed into pubs and cosy country hotels. Game reserves have been established, their mission being to restock indigenous animals and protect them for the benefit of future generations.

It's a special pleasure to see the herds multiplying and running free, to dine in characterful restaurants serving local specialities, and to sleep in rooms where early settlers dreamed of peace and posterity.

HOUT BAY HARBOUR IS A BUSTLE OF ACTIVITY DURING THE ANNUAL WINTER 'SNOEK RUN' AND LOCALS RUSH TO THE WATER'S EDGE TO BUY FRESH FISH TO BRAAI.

seafood

CREATURES THAT SWIM, crawl and cling to wave-washed rocks have been caught in southern seas since the mists of time. Ancient middens and relics of primitive fish traps prove that Strandlopers were masters of the art of ferreting out nourishment from the sea. However, due to the similarity between fish and snakes, seafood is not part of the traditional black diet, though some coastal-dwellers like the Tsonga and Xhosa trap and spear fish and collect shellfish, and use the shells as spoons and pot scrapers.

Most of the Dutch fish names were bestowed by Jan van Riebeeck, whose soldiers were fed so much fish there was once talk of mutiny! The Governor's response was to extend the rations to include the meat and eggs of penguins and other seabirds.

Fishing skills had to be learned, however, as Europeans were relatively ignorant in this regard. But they soon enjoyed such fishy feasts as perlemoen (abalone), alikreukels and black and white mussels. Some creatures – octopus, sea urchins, periwinkles, limpets and the like – never featured prominently on the Cape table, though a rich soup was made by scrubbing and soaking limpets in water, then crushing (shells and all) and simmering in water with onions, garlic, seaweed and peppercorns. The strained broth was thickened with flour and finished with a dash of sherry.

Though delicious, octopus and redbait were – and still are – most often used as bait, as was chokka (squid, also known as calamari), prolific in eastern Cape waters. This is now exported in huge quantities, and snaffled up by local restaurants.

There was a fish market in a sandy cove at the bottom of Adderley Street in Cape Town where folk gathered to wait for fishing boats to return with the fresh catch of the day. Kalk Bay and Hout Bay harbours served those who lived in the southern peninsula.

Fish became a source of Government revenue in the late 1700s. Steam-driven trawlers sailed from Simon's Town and other coastal places. On their return, fresh fish would be sold by the bunch to Cape Malay vendors, who slung fish-filled baskets on bamboo yokes over their shoulders, and peddled their wares from door to door. At the sound of their fish horns, kitchen maids and cooks would run out to purchase fresh fish.

Horns were first made of hollow kelp found washed up on the beach; later they were fashioned from paraffin tins, while fish carts replaced foot-slogging vendors. Eventually, with the advent of modern supermarkets the call of the fish horn was silenced forever.

fish frikkadels with rougail

Frikkadels – a lovely old-fashioned word – refers both to fishcakes and meatballs. Big, fat ones are fab for dinner, while smaller ones are good with pre-prandial drinks. Fish frikkadels may be flavoured in various ways; here we have an Indian spin. Any fish can be used, freshly-cooked for the occasion, left-over from a baked or braaied beastie – even tinned salmon, tuna or pilchards if all else fails. Rougail – a salady garnish of Tamil origin that has made its home in the Indian Ocean islands – rounds things off gloriously.

makes about 12; serves 4 to 6

500g smoked or cooked fish fillets
300g potatoes, peeled and diced
60ml chopped coriander
2 eggs, lightly beaten
salt and milled black pepper
juice of 1 lemon or lime
250ml toasted breadcrumbs
2 limes, to serve
vegetable oil

ROUGAIL
3–4 spring onions, finely chopped
3 roma or plum tomatoes, chopped
60ml chopped coriander
salt and milled black pepper
olive oil
lime juice

Skin and flake the fish. Cook the potatoes in a saucepan of salted boiling water. Drain well and mash. Mix in the fish, coriander and egg, and flavour with salt and pepper and a good squeeze of lemon or lime juice. Shape into patties, flattening them between your palms. Coat with toasted crumbs.

Cut the limes in half, brush generously with oil and grill in a frying pan until lightly charred and smoky.

ROUGAIL Mix together the spring onions, tomatoes and coriander, and season with salt and pepper. Add a little olive oil and lime juice. Spoon into a bowl.

Heat oil in a medium frying pan for shallow-frying, and fry the frikkadels until crisp and golden; 2 or 3 minutes on each side should do it.

Serve hot or at room temperature – never chilled, as they lose all their flavour. Rougail and charred limes can be presented alongside or in separate bowls.

smoorvis is typical of
many recipes that are
deeply rooted in culture,
history and rituals.

SMOORVIS

'Smothered fish' was originally prepared with fish preserved by salt and drying in sea breezes. After soaking in water to get rid of excess salt, the flesh was flaked and mixed with spicy rice. Smoked fish – usually snoek – is more often used today, though any smoked fish would be fine. For centuries South Africans have prepared similar dishes using ingredients as diverse as crayfish and hard-boiled chicken or penguin eggs, crabs and mussels. It's delicious for breakfast, lunch or dinner with brown bread and atjar or Blatjang (page 161) (chutney).

serves 6

500g smoked fish
100g uncooked long-grain rice
250ml water
salt and milled black pepper
butter and vegetable oil
2 onions, finely sliced
2 potatoes, peeled and cut into
   small dice
2 slices green ginger, peeled
1 red or green chilli, finely sliced
   and seeded
2 large, ripe tomatoes, blanched,
   peeled and chopped
lemon juice

Bone, skin and roughly flake the fish. Tip the rice into a medium saucepan with the water and 5ml salt, cover and cook for about 20 minutes until the rice is cooked and the water has been absorbed.

Heat a generous amount of butter and oil in a large frying pan and fry the onions until translucent. Add the potatoes and fry until golden. Stir in the ginger, chilli and tomatoes, and cook over more gentle heat for a few minutes more. Stir occasionally.

Mix in the fish and rice, cover and steam over low heat until the smoorvis is piping hot and the potato is cooked. Check the flavour and add lemon juice and pepper, and a little salt if necessary. You may find, though, that the fish is sufficiently salty in the first place. Serve directly from the pan or tip into a warm dish and serve hot.

penang fish

Many Cape Malays came from the island of Penang, a historic port at the northern end of the Straits of Malacca in Malaysia. Recipes from there inspired many dishes that are now firmly ensconced in our repertoire.

serves 6

1kg filleted white fish
10ml tamarind paste
60ml hot water
Ghee (page 215), or butter and vegetable oil
1 onion, finely sliced
10ml curry powder
2 garlic cloves, crushed
small knob green ginger, peeled and crushed
4 ripe tomatoes, peeled and chopped, or 400g tin
   whole peeled tomatoes, chopped in their juice
15ml lemon juice
salt and milled black pepper
250ml coconut cream
125ml Fish Stock (page 216)

Skin the fish and cut into large pieces. Soften the tamarind in hot water for about 10 minutes.

Heat a little ghee or butter and oil in a large frying pan and fry the onion until golden. Stir in the curry powder, garlic, ginger, tomatoes, lemon juice and tamarind (with the water), and season with salt and pepper.

Pour in the coconut cream and stock. Cover and simmer over low heat for 10 minutes. Nestle the fish pieces into the sauce, cover and simmer for about 6 minutes until cooked. The cooking time will depend on the thickness of the fish. Serve hot with rice or potatoes.

masaLa fish

This Eastern dish – similarly recorded by both Indian and Cape Malay food writers – is great whatever fish you use, but make sure it's fresh.

serves 6

1kg filleted white fish (skin on)
salt and milled black pepper
2 garlic cloves
1 green chilli, seeded
30ml vegetable oil, plus extra for frying
juice of ½ lemon
5ml ground cumin
5ml ground coriander
2ml turmeric
lemon wedges, for squeezing
Chilli Jam (page 160), to serve

Cut the fish into serving portions, and season with a little salt and pepper. Pound together the garlic and chilli with a pestle and mortar. Mix in the oil, lemon juice, cumin, coriander and turmeric. Pour into a flat dish and add the fish, flesh side down. Set aside for about 1 hour.

Heat a little oil in a large frying pan and fry the fish over medium heat for 3 to 4 minutes on each side until done. Serve with lemon wedges for squeezing, and a little chilli jam on the side.

kyLa's pickLed fish

This is an old family recipe that my mother-in-law taught me when I was newly-married. Her grandchildren affectionately called her 'Kyla'. In the early 1800s the Green Point Common on the outskirts of Cape Town was a racecourse, where folk met twice a year for a day of sport and culinary delights such a suckling pig, braaied snoek, watermelon konfyt and pickled fish. The recipe was created by the Cape Malays, expert fishermen who are adept at preserving their catch to make it last as long as possible. Firm-fleshed yellowtail and snoek are favoured, but other fish may be substituted – even humble hake.

SERVES 8 TO 10

1,7–2kg filleted fish (2,5–3kg on the bone)
vegetable oil
150g sultanas (optional)

PICKLING SAUCE
750ml white wine vinegar
250ml water
150g sugar
10ml turmeric
10ml Roasted Masala (page 213), or curry powder
7ml salt
15ml black peppercorns
15ml coriander seeds
4 onions, finely sliced
6 lemon or bay leaves
2 green or red chillies, sliced and seeded
6 slices green ginger, peeled
30ml cornflour
125ml water

Cut the fish into cubes or slices. Heat oil in a large frying pan for shallow-frying, and fry the fish until cooked. Drain on kitchen paper. Remove the skin.

PICKLING SAUCE Combine the vinegar, water, sugar, turmeric, masala or curry powder, salt, peppercorns and coriander in a large saucepan. Bring to the boil, stirring to dissolve the sugar.

Add the onions, lemon or bay leaves, chillies and ginger, cover and simmer for 10 to 12 minutes. The onion should be limp but still slightly crunchy. Mix together the cornflour and water and add to the boiling sauce, stirring until it thickens slightly.

Layer the fish, sultanas and onion in a large non-metal dish, pour over the sauce, cover and refrigerate. Pickled fish may be eaten immediately; however the flavour is even better after a couple of days. Firm fish will keep for up to six months in the fridge; delicate types such as kob, geelbek or hake may be kept for two months.

PICKLED fish, a favourite at festivals and feasts, eloquently HIGHLIGHTS the impact that eastern influences have had on cuisine at the southern tip of africa.

BLack mussels in curry cream

Black mussel shells have been found in the middens of early coastal-dwelling hunter-gatherers, which points to their popularity for many centuries. This is a modern version of a classic old Cape recipe.

serves 6

36 black mussels, well scrubbed
250ml water or dry white wine
butter and vegetable oil
1 onion, finely chopped
3 garlic cloves, crushed
5ml Roasted Masala (page 213), or curry powder
2ml turmeric
125ml cream
60ml chopped coriander

Carefully pull out the mussel beards and place the mussels in a medium saucepan with the water or wine. Cover and boil for about 5 minutes until they open. Discard any that remain shut. Lift the mussels from the pan and set aside. Strain the mussel liquor.

Heat a generous amount of butter and oil in a large frying pan and fry the onion until golden. Add the garlic, masala or curry powder and turmeric. Pour in the mussel liquor and cream, and boil uncovered until the sauce thickens slightly.

Just before serving, add the mussels and coriander to the sauce and heat through.

mussel-gathering from the rocks at low tide is loads of fun. they should be served as fresh as possible, no longer than a day after being plucked from their watery home. keep chilled between gathering and cooking.

kommetjie crayfish

The eagerly-anticipated crayfish season each summer sees fishermen heading out to sea in anything that floats to catch their quota. Our favourite spot is Kommetjie, a small fishing village on the Cape Peninsula. To complement the convivial mood, recipes for this seductive shellfish must be easy, casual and quite delicious. This dish fits all these criteria; there are no complicated ingredients, and the cooking procedure is spontaneous. Lemongrass, popular in Malaysian, Vietnamese and Thai cooking, is the dominant flavour in this glorious recipe that combines frying and steaming; perfect for cooking crayfish.

serves 2

2 crayfish
1 stalk lemongrass
butter and olive oil
4 garlic cloves
60ml chopped parsley
lemon juice
salt and milled black pepper
lemon wedges, for squeezing
fennel fronds, for garnishing

Cut the crayfish in half through the carapace and tail shell. Pull out and discard the alimentary canals. Remove the hard outer leaves of the lemongrass and slice the core finely.

Heat a large knob of butter and a little olive oil in a frying pan and fry the crayfish, flesh down, until nicely browned. This will only take a couple of minutes. Add the sliced lemongrass, garlic, parsley and a generous squeeze of lemon juice.

Turn the crayfish over, cover the pan and steam over medium heat for about 5 minutes until cooked through. Season lightly with salt and pepper.

Serve directly from the pan or lift onto a platter with lemon wedges for squeezing and fennel fronds for an extra touch of colour. Pour the pan juices into a bowl and offer separately.

oLives & ostriches; koppies & campfire tales

the karoo & northern cape

9

SOUTHERN AFRICA'S SUN-BAKED KAROOS ARE AMONG THE MOST SPACIOUS PLATEAUX IN THE WORLD. FLAT-TOPPED HILLOCKS DOT THE LANDSCAPE. TUMBLEWEEDS TUMBLE ALONG ON THEIR MAD JOURNEY TO WHO KNOWS WHERE. THE AIR IS FRESH, THE SUN SETS IN AN ALMOST INDECENT FLOODING OF COLOUR AND NIGHT SKIES ARE LIT BY A MILLION BRILLIANT STARS.

Whether passing through, or staying awhile, your perspective of time, distance and the tenacity of man shifts, for it's hard to imagine anyone surviving in such a harsh, lonely terrain. Yet these were once rich hunting grounds of the San.

As in many isolated places of the world where man has struggled for survival, food – now as then – is all the more precious for its scarcity. Sustenance came from the meat of antelope, zebra, elephant and buffalo. Veldkos included wild bulbs, fruits and berries, roots and tubers and leaves and seeds of bushes. Wild honey was collected; nectar was gathered from red aloes.

Nineteenth-century trek-farmers lived off the land as well; kelkiewyn (Namaqua partridges) were simmered in potjies; bredies were prepared with gourds; kambro bulbs were made into jam and served as a vegetable. Venison was smoked and roasted – dishes far removed from the spice-fragrant Western Cape fare of the time.

Hollowed-out ant heaps became ovens for baking bread, puddings, pies and vegetables such as pumpkin and patat (sweet potato). Fruit from the rosyntjiebos (raisin bush) was crushed and made into brandy for an after dinner soet-soepie (sweet drink).

Karoo food was called skoff (cuisine is far too posh a term), derived from Dutch sailors' schaften or noon meal. Skof is also Afrikaans for stage (or trek), indicating the meal at the end of a journey.

Klein (Little) Karoo plains are cradled in rugged mountain ranges forming a natural buffer from the coastal terrace. It wasn't until 1689 that the first whites managed the journey through the kloofs. The San called the area Kannaland after a wild bush; other names included 'land of thirst' and 'karo' meaning dry.

Today small farming communities grow potatoes, figs, olives, apples, pears, peaches and apricots. Brandy is distilled; cheese is made. Wines come from the Breede River Valley and towns such as Robertson and Montagu, particularly sweet Muscadel and Muscat d'Alexandrie (known locally as Hanepoot).

In Graaff-Reinet, 'the gem of the Karoo', old buildings are restored to maintain the gracious nineteenth-century atmosphere. The town is surrounded by the Karoo Nature Reserve, watched over by Spandau Kop mountain and not far from the Valley of Desolation – our oldest National Monument.

The Cango Valley, famous for the Cango Caves, is home of the ostrich, an ungainly, foul-tempered bird. San hunters in search of eggs disguised themselves with ostrich skins over their backs and one arm held aloft to resemble the bird's long neck. One egg is equivalent to twenty-four hen's eggs and takes about an hour to boil.

The Oudtshoorn ostrich market peaked in about 1882 when feathers adorned French show girls and American high society ladies. At home feathers were put to more mundane purposes – dusting homes and swatting flies. In the 1990s ostrich meat attained international acclaim. Although a red meat similar to beef in taste and texture, ostrich has virtually no fat and a vestige of cholesterol.

Karoo lamb is famous for its succulence and flavour. Merinos feast on wild rosemary, Karoo bush, brakbos and gannabos. Legs are roasted; chops are braaied; shoulders are baked. Chubby tails of the Blackhead Persian render fat for cooking and baking. Bits of crisp, salted fat, called kaaiings (crackling), and toutjiesvleis (string-like biltong strips) are popular snacks.

Earlier specialities include offal bobotie, tripe with chopped liver, and large intestines braaied over the coals. Offal cakes (pannas) were prepared with tripe and trotters spiced with cloves, nutmeg, coriander and black pepper. Gullets were stuffed with prickly pear, which grow throughout the Little Karoo. During the 1930s the fruit and leaves were made into preserves, syrup, atjar and beer.

BELOW LEFT: *The peaceful hamlet of Prince Albert in the Great Karoo.*

BELOW RIGHT: *Flocks of sheep are a common sight when one is travelling through the Karoo.*

ABOVE: *Ostriches are farmed for their meat, feathers and eggs, each one equivalent to twenty-four hen's eggs.*

FAR LEFT: *A field of* Aloe striata *flower near Steytlerville.*

LEFT: *Brightly coloured aloes are a feature of the landscape as you travel through the Karoo.*

OPPOSITE: *A herd of blesbok graze peacefully in the Karoo National Park.*

The semi-desert Great Karoo abuts the Small Karoo and is bordered by southern mountain ranges – the Hex River, Swartberg, Baviaanskloof, Great Winterhoek and Suurberg. In the west are Namaqualand, the Cederberg and Lower Bokkeveld. The Orange River forms the northern boundary. Southerly migrating Hottentots named the plains 'garob' – which means dry, unfruitful and uninhabited rolled into one.

In the Northern Cape, encircled by the dust-dry upper Karoo, southern Kalahari and Namaqualand highlands, there's a thriving farming community in the lush Orange River Valley. The river rises 2000 kilometres away in Lesotho, crashes into the Augrabies gorge near Upington, then flows on to form our boundary with Namibia on its journey to the Atlantic Ocean.

River banks are lined with date palms, pomegranate trees, orange groves, fruit orchards, vegetable patches, and vast fields of cotton and lucerne. Vineyards stretch as far as the eye can see, the fruit destined for drying and turning into wine. Some of the first hand-built irrigation canals still zigzag through the countryside.

Kalahari truffles, one of Africa's most unusual delicacies, are indigenous to the Northern Cape. They grow in deep cracks of the red desert sand. Some are thumb-sized; others are as large as an apple. Simply steamed and seasoned, truffles are insipid, but their fragrance is a wonderful flavour enhancer for other ingredients.

This vast region appeals to those who're keen to swap urban stress for rural bliss, and who enjoy the starkness of sun-baked plains, having space to spare and listening to campfire tales. Farmhouses have been turned into homely bed-and-breakfast establishments and guest houses. There are stoeps to lounge on, fireplaces to ward off winter's chill, and high ceilings to cool the heat of summer.

Even though the plains no longer thunder with the hoofs of antelope, areas once over-grazed by sheep are being gradually restocked with game. Though veldkos is getting scarcer and skills required in its preparation are dying out, those who know where to find it gather it wisely and prepare it well.

If home is, as they say, where the heart is, homely, hearty Karoo skoff will be around a while longer.

master butcher steve jeffery trims man-sized t-bone steaks for his customers at the neighbourgoods market in woodstock near cape town.

meat

CHAPTER TEN

THE AFRICAN SAVANNAH ONCE TEEMED WITH PLAINS GAME. Hunters bagged antelope, lion, elephant, rhinoceros and hippos, and smaller animals like jackals, ostriches, hares, hedgehogs and mice.

Settlers learned hunting skills from residents of the land they now called home, for in Europe hunting – for larger game at least – was reserved for the nobility. Even so, providing sufficient fresh meat for ships passing the Cape of Good Hope was a problem. The long sea journey hampered the importing of breeding stock and, as neither Strandlopers nor San owned sheep or cattle, meat was bartered from Hottentots to the north.

Dassies, seagulls and penguins (and their eggs) appeared on the Cape table. Later pigs were imported and sheep were bred. Joints of mutton or venison were larded with bacon, steeped in vinegar flavoured with cloves, lemon leaves, thyme, peppercorns and coriander, then rubbed with flour, topped with lard and roasted. Modern cooks seldom marinate venison and avoid adding lard, though studding with bacon still imparts succulence and extra flavour.

Meat is viewed differently in various cultures. In tribal communities, for example, cooking methods are simplest – boiling or roasting over the fire – and strict religious and ancestral customs dictate both slaughtering and portioning. Cape Malays, on the other hand, enjoy spicy dishes, and follow the teachings of Islam, which dictates which food may and may not be eaten. Cape Dutch recipes are plainer.

Though never considered a status food, offal (or afvalkos) has always been popular on South African menus. French Huguenots fine-tuned offal recipes, influencing the preparation of meat, lightening up on both the flavouring and the amount of fat used.

With urbanization and the gradual taming of the continent, wild meats made way for domesticated livestock – long considered the measure of the status of tribal folk. Nowadays few men hunt for the pot and our recipes are more likely to have an international bias. However, for times when comfort-zone fare is called for, we enjoy looking over our shoulder. You'll find meat recipes here that are simple and straightforward, and inspired equally by our forebears as well as the rest of the African continent.

west african peanut chicken

Coconut and peanuts (groundnuts) are popular throughout Africa as well as in neighbouring Indian Ocean islands such as Madagascar, Seychelles and Comores. Add that fabulous foursome of garlic, ginger, turmeric and chilli and bags of fresh thyme and you have a dish that seduces the taste buds. It's even better next day, so prepare it ahead and reheat gently.

serves 4 to 6

8 chicken drumsticks
salt and milled black pepper
vegetable oil
2 onions, sliced
1 red or green chilli, sliced and seeded
2ml turmeric
leaves from a small bunch thyme
400g tin whole peeled tomatoes, chopped in their juice
250ml cream
250ml Chicken Stock (page 216)
100g roasted and salted peanuts, roughly chopped

Skin the chicken and season with salt and pepper. Heat a little oil in a large saucepan and lightly brown the chicken all over. Remove from the pan and set aside.

Add the onions to the pan (with a little extra oil if necessary) and braise over medium heat until golden. Add the chilli, turmeric, thyme, tomatoes, cream, stock and half the peanuts. Return the chicken to the pan, cover and simmer over very gentle heat for about 30 minutes until cooked.

Lift the chicken onto a warm serving dish. If necessary, boil the sauce uncovered to thicken it a little, then pour over the chicken. Garnish with the remaining peanuts and serve with rice.

cape chicken curry

Malay curries have a glorious complexity of flavours and are always more gently spiced than Indian curries. An early scribe described chicken curry as 'a fowl cut up in small pieces' and simmered with sliced onion, chillies, turmeric, coriander seeds, cumin and coconut milk.

serves 4 to 6

8 chicken thighs
salt and milled black pepper
vegetable oil
2 onions, roughly chopped
2 garlic cloves, finely chopped
small knob ginger, peeled and finely chopped
2 cassia or cinnamon sticks
15ml Roasted Masala (page 213), or curry powder
5ml turmeric
5ml ground cumin
5ml ground coriander
2ml ground cardamom
400g tin whole peeled tomatoes, chopped in their juice
410ml tin coconut cream
coriander leaves, for garnishing

Skin the chicken and season with salt and pepper. Heat a little oil in a large saucepan and fry the onions until golden. Stir in the garlic, ginger, cassia or cinnamon, masala or curry powder, turmeric, cumin, coriander and cardamom. Simmer for about 15 seconds to release the flavours (don't let the spices burn). Add the tomatoes and coconut cream.

Nestle the chicken thighs into the sauce, cover and simmer for about 40 minutes until cooked. Transfer the curry to a warm serving dish, garnish with coriander and serve with rice and a selection of sambals.

a shortage of milk in the javanese homeland of cape malays encouraged them to substitute coconut cream. as a result, it was introduced to a variety of early cape dishes like this gloriously-flavoured chicken curry photographed below.

chicken pie

Pies were all the rage in Holland in the eighteenth century, and their popularity spread far and wide. They were among the earliest bakes sold by the 'free bakers' in the Cape Colony. Hoenderpastei (chicken pie) is associated with celebrations – Christmas, birthdays and Cape Malay wedding feasts. Free-range chickens are the birds of choice, just as they were before the advent of battery-reared chickens.

serves 6

1 chicken
1 litre Chicken Stock (page 216)
1 onion, roughly chopped
10 black peppercorns
3 whole cloves
2ml ground allspice or mixed spice
salt and milled black pepper
30ml sago
2 egg yolks, lightly beaten
lemon juice
200g ham, diced (optional)
400g puff pastry
1 egg
15ml milk

Place the chicken in a large saucepan with the stock, onion, peppercorns, cloves and allspice or mixed spice. Cover, bring to the boil, then reduce the heat and simmer for about 50 minutes until the chicken is cooked.

Lift the chicken from the stock and discard the skin and bones. Break the meat into small pieces and season with salt and pepper.

Boil the stock uncovered until reduced by half and slightly thickened. Add the sago, cover and simmer for about 15 minutes until transparent. Remove from the stove and stir in the egg yolks to make a creamy sauce. Flavour with a good squeeze of lemon juice and a little salt and pepper.

Mix the chicken meat and diced ham into the sauce. Spoon into a buttered pie dish or six smaller dishes for individual servings. Cool to room temperature.

Heat the oven to 200°C. Unroll the pastry, cover the pie/s and make a hole in the centre to allow the steam to escape. Mix together the egg and milk and brush onto the pastry. Bake for about 20 minutes until the filling is hot and the pastry is crisply golden.

UNLIKE MORE CUMBERSOME VERSIONS OF BREYANI, THIS ONE IS RELATIVELY QUICK TO DO.

chicken breyani

There are many different ways of preparing this famous South Asian dish that has a special place in the hearts of South African cooks, especially Indians and Cape Malays. There are various ways of spelling it, too, as well as spices that may be added. Here's my favourite recipe, which is an adaptation of many I have tried. The special joy of a breyani is the smell that wafts through the house as the lid is lifted.

serves 6 to 8

12 skinless, filleted chicken thighs

salt and milled black pepper

250ml plain yoghurt

5ml Green Masala (page 213)

2ml turmeric

2ml ground cumin

2ml ground coriander

125ml brown lentils

500ml water

Ghee (page 215), or butter and vegetable oil

2 onions, sliced

2 cinnamon sticks

6 cardamom pods, lightly crushed

250ml uncooked basmati rice

375ml Chicken Stock (page 216)

4 hard-boiled eggs (optional)

coriander leaves, for garnishing

Heat the oven to 200°C. Place the chicken in a bowl and season with salt and pepper. Mix together the yoghurt, masala, turmeric, cumin and coriander, pour over the chicken and toss to mix everything together well.

Place the lentils in a medium saucepan with the water, cover and simmer for 20 minutes. Drain.

Heat a generous amount of ghee or butter and oil in a large casserole and fry the onions until golden. Add the cinnamon and cardamom and sizzle for about 15 seconds until aromatic. Stir in the rice and lentils. Add the stock and season with salt and pepper.

Remove the pan from the heat. Nestle the chicken into the breyani, cover and bake for about 40 minutes until the chicken is cooked and the rice has absorbed all the stock. Garnish with halved hard-boiled eggs and coriander, and serve with Blatjang (page 161).

pot-roast chicken with dates

Dates team up marvellously with chicken. Most of our fresh and dried dates are imported, but some come from the lush Orange River basin in the Upington area of the North West Province. Make sure your pot has a well-fitting lid to keep in all the moisture and flavour from the chicken. This mingles magically with the flavours you're adding to the pot, forming an utterly delicious gravy. If needs be, place a double layer of heavy foil between pot and lid. This dish cooks itself, so there's no need to pfaff around with it when you have other things to do.

serves 5 to 6

1 chicken

salt and milled black pepper

butter and vegetable oil

1 onion, finely chopped

1 cinnamon stick

6 whole cloves

125ml Chicken Stock (page 216)

125ml medium dry sherry

30ml honey

15ml dijon mustard

finely grated zest of 1 orange

200g dates, fresh or dried

Wash and dry the chicken and season inside and out with salt and pepper. Heat a generous amount of butter and oil in a large saucepan and brown the bird lightly all over. Remove from the pan and set aside.

Stir the onion into the pan juices and braise over medium-high heat until lightly browned. Stir in the cinnamon and cloves, then add the stock, sherry, honey, mustard and orange zest. Nestle the chicken into the sauce, cover and simmer very gently for about 30 minutes. Add the dates (if they're dried), and continue pot-roasting until the chicken is done; about 30 minutes more should do it. If using fresh dates, add to the pan about 5 minutes before the end of cooking.

Lift the chicken and dates from the pan and place on a platter. Check the gravy and, if necessary, boil uncovered until reduced, thickened and absolutely delicious. Pour over the chicken, or offer separately in a jug.

it's important to use a pot with a well-fitting lid to keep in all the moisture and nudge every drop of flavour from the chicken.

the secrets of a
great bredie lie
in well-browned
meat and onions,
balanced spicing
and smooring
('smothering') long
and slow until the
meat falls from the
bones and all the
ingredients merge
together.

tomato bredie

Bredies were introduced by Eastern slaves, and include ingredients like cabbage, beetroot, spinach, sorrel and Karoo veldkool (veld cabbage). Pumpkin, water-blommetjies and green beans are other variations. The name, though, comes from Madagascar, an island with strong trade links with India and Malaysia. Use very little additional liquid in tomato bredie, as the intense flavour should come from the meat and tomatoes – always fresh and ripened to the peak of sweet perfection. It's important to have a pot with a well-fitting lid, or a cast-iron potjie if you're cooking your bredie over the coals. Bredies are even better prepared a day or two ahead and reheated.

serves 6

1kg lamb knuckle

salt and milled black pepper

cake flour

vegetable oil

2 onions, sliced

3 garlic cloves, crushed

small knob green ginger, peeled
    and crushed

5ml ground coriander

2ml ground cardamom

2ml ground fennel

leaves from a small bunch thyme

30ml chopped marjoram

1kg very ripe tomatoes, blanched,
    skinned and chopped

10ml brown sugar

Trim the meat. Season with salt and pepper, and dredge lightly with flour. Heat a little oil in a large saucepan and brown the meat. Remove from the pan and set aside. Add the onions, garlic and ginger to the pan juices and braise over medium-high heat until the onion turns a rich golden brown. Stir occasionally.

Return the meat to the pan. Add the coriander, cardamom, fennel, thyme, marjoram and tomatoes, and brown sugar to balance the acidity of the tomatoes. Cover and simmer over very gentle heat for about 1½ hours until the meat is as tender as can be. Stir occasionally and check the consistency; add a little water only if it's absolutely necessary.

Serve with plain rice or boiled potatoes and Quince Sambal (page 156). If waterblommetjies are in season, serve them as well, simply steamed and flavoured with lemon juice, salt and pepper.

DENNINGVLEIS

This recipe is one of the courses served at a Batavian rijstafel, brought from Java by the Malays. The name means 'flavoured meat' and the recipe has its origins in the Javanese 'dendeng', a dish originally prepared with the meat of water buffalo which was cured with salt and spices, dried in the sun and fried in coconut oil. Tamarind – the pasty dried fruit of an Indian tree – is the traditional flavouring. If you can't find it, substitute a dash of good wine vinegar or a squeeze of lemon, which lend a similar sourish note.

serves 6 to 8

1,5 kg lamb leg or knuckle

vegetable oil

4 onions, roughly chopped

4 garlic cloves, crushed

5ml grated nutmeg

2ml ground allspice

6 whole cloves

2 bay leaves

salt and milled black pepper

375ml hot water

10ml tamarind paste

Trim the lamb and cut into chunks. Brown in hot oil in a large saucepan a few pieces at a time. Remove from the pan and set aside. Add the onions and garlic, and fry gently until translucent. Return the meat to the pan with the nutmeg, allspice, cloves, bay leaves and a little salt and pepper.

Pour in a cupful of hot water, cover and simmer very gently until the lamb is tender; this will take 60 to 90 minutes. Add more water from time to time if necessary.

Soak the tamarind in a little of the hot sauce and add to the pot about 10 minutes before the end of the cooking time. Serve with Yellow Rice (page 65).

Lamb Roghan Josh

Indian dishes like this one have an extraordinary alchemy of ingredients which gives diners the experience of layers of flavours unfolding in the eating. Recipes are usually passed down by example from mother to daughter, rather than by the written word.

serves 6

SPICE MIXTURE
10ml ground coriander
5ml ground cumin
5ml poppy seeds
2ml ground fennel
2ml ground cardamom
2ml milled black pepper
2ml turmeric
1ml ground cloves

ROGHAN JOSH
1,5kg lamb leg
Ghee (page 215), or butter and vegetable oil
1 onion, chopped
1–2 green or red chillies, sliced and seeded
6 garlic cloves, crushed
small knob green ginger, peeled and finely chopped
30ml desiccated coconut
50g slivered almonds
4 cardamom pods, lightly crushed
400g tin whole peeled tomatoes, chopped in their juice
7ml salt
5ml Garam Masala (page 214)
125ml plain yoghurt

SPICE MIXTURE   Mix together all the spices.

ROGHAN JOSH   Trim the lamb and cut into chunks. Heat a little ghee or butter and oil in a large saucepan and fry the onion until golden. Add the meat and stir until lightly browned.

Add the chilli, garlic, ginger, coconut, almonds and cardamom. Stir in the spice mixture, tomatoes and salt.

Cover and simmer very gently until the meat is tender, stirring occasionally. The cooking time may vary from 1 to 1½ hours depending on the meat. Sprinkle with garam masala, stir in and cook for 5 minutes more. Stir in the yoghurt and heat through.

Transfer the roghan josh into a warm serving bowl and serve with plain rice or Yellow Rice (page 65).

Lamb tagine with chickpeas and mango

Tagines are wonderfully forgiving to prepare; once they're in the oven they pretty much get on with it while you're doing something else. Cooking time isn't watch-the-clock stuff either; you're aiming for the moment when the meat is falling-off-the-bone tender and all the other ingredients have melted into an intensely personal relationship with each other. Like a really warm hug.

serves 6

1kg lamb knuckle

olive oil

salt and milled black pepper

2 onions, thickly sliced

250ml Beef Stock (page 217)

400g tin whole peeled tomatoes,
    chopped in their juice

10ml ground cumin

5ml ground coriander

2ml ground ginger

2ml ground cinnamon

400g tin chickpeas, drained

125g sun-dried mango strips

30ml chopped mint

45ml chopped coriander

Heat the oven to 160°C. Trim the meat. Heat a little olive oil in a large frying pan and seal the meat over medium-high heat. Remove the meat from the pan and place in the tagine (or your casserole of choice). Season with salt and pepper.

Add the onions to the frying pan (with a little more oil if necessary) and fry until golden brown. Place on the meat. Pour the stock into the pan, then add the tomatoes, cumin, coriander, ginger and cinnamon. Stir up all the brown bits in the pan and season with salt and pepper. Pour over the onions. Cover the tagine or casserole and bake in the oven until the meat is so tender it falls from the bones. This should take about 1½ hours, depending on the cut.

Mix the chickpeas, mango, mint and coriander into the sauce, cover and bake for about 10 minutes more until the chickpeas are hot and the mango has plumped up nicely. Whip off the lid and garnish the tagine generously with extra mint and coriander, if you wish. Serve piping hot.

NORTH AFRICAN TAGINES ARE THE ULTIMATE SLOW FOOD — SPICE-FRAGRANT, GENTLY-COOKED MEAT, FISH AND VEGETABLE DISHES OF COUNTRIES LIKE ALGIERS, MOROCCO AND TUNISIA.

meat frikkadels with tomato smoor

The Dutch introduced meatballs to our menu, and they're flavoured in many different ways. To make cabbage frikkadels, also known as 'oumens onder die kombers' (old people under the blanket), wrap the meatballs in blanched cabbage leaves and simmer in a pan of beef stock for about 30 minutes.

serves 6

800g minced beef or lamb,
　or a mixture of the two
1 onion, finely chopped
60ml chopped parsley
5ml ground coriander
2ml ground cloves
5ml salt, milled black pepper
2 slices bread, crumbled
125ml milk
1 egg, lightly beaten

TOMATO SMOOR
vegetable oil
2 onions, finely chopped
4 large, ripe tomatoes, blanched,
　peeled and chopped, or 400g tin
　whole peeled tomatoes,
　chopped in their juice
60ml chopped herbs (parsley,
　thyme, oregano)
15ml brown sugar
1ml paprika

Mix together the mince, onion, parsley, coriander, cloves, salt and pepper in a bowl. Place the bread in another bowl, pour over the milk, and add to the mince with the egg. Mix everything together and form into about 16 balls.

TOMATO SMOOR Heat plenty of oil in a medium saucepan and braise the onions over medium heat for about 10 minutes until very soft and well browned. Don't rush the process, as the onion should be deliciously caramelized. Add the remaining ingredients, season with salt and pepper, and cook briskly uncovered, stirring occasionally. Within 8 to 10 minutes the sauce will be beautifully thick. Check the flavour and adjust if necessary.

Heat oil in a large frying pan for shallow-frying and fry the meatballs for 10 to 12 minutes until almost cooked through, turning frequently so they brown evenly. Take care that the oil isn't too hot; they may burn before the middles are cooked.

Drain the meatballs on kitchen paper, pile onto a warm plate and spoon tomato smoor over.

this recipe comes from the heart of the karoo, where lamb is plentiful. you're welcome to use rosemary instead of lavender if you prefer.

Leg of Lamb with Lavender

Long ago Hottentots dwelt in the Karoo with fat-tailed sheep. Later the 1820 British Settlers introduced merinos, hardy sheep that fed on aromatic wild veld bushes and grew fat and tasty. Olden-day lamb recipes were extremely rich as they were pot-roasted in their own fat, or the fat of the tail. Under-cooked lamb is seldom found locally; we prefer lamb cooked long and slow until it practically falls from the bone.

serves 8

1 leg of lamb (about 2kg)
salt and milled black pepper
500ml buttermilk
finely grated zest and juice of 1 lemon
125ml olive oil
peeled cloves from 1 head of garlic
60ml finely chopped lavender leaves
large bunch lavender
30ml cornflour
250ml cream
60ml medium dry sherry

Place the lamb in a roaster and season with salt and pepper. Mix together the buttermilk, lemon zest and juice, olive oil, garlic cloves and chopped lavender and pour over. Set aside at room temperature for 3 to 4 hours (or refrigerate overnight if you have the time).

Heat the oven to 200°C. Place the lavender bunch on top of the meat, cover with foil and roast for 30 minutes. Reduce the oven temperature to 160°C and roast for a further 2 hours or until the lamb is very tender.

Transfer the lamb to a clean roaster. Increase the oven heat to 220°C and roast uncovered for about 20 minutes to brown the meat while finishing the sauce.

Mix together the cornflour, cream and sherry, and add to the pan juices. Mash the garlic cloves into the sauce and whisk until smooth and thickened (buttermilk has a tendency to separate while the lamb roasts).

Place the lamb on a carving board and garnish with fresh lavender. Offer the sauce separately.

BOBOTIE

This is South Africa's unofficial – and much loved – national dish: spiced minced meat with a savoury custard topping. The name is derived from the Indonesian bobotok, indicating that the recipe has its roots in the Dutch East India Company colonies in Batavia. A similar dish was known in Europe in the Middle Ages after the Crusaders had brought turmeric from the East. After South Africans settled in other African countries, bobotie now features on menus in Zimbabwe, Kenya, Botswana and Zambia. Bobotie should be tender and creamy in texture, which calls for long, slow cooking.

serves 8

butter and vegetable oil

2 onions, finely chopped

1kg minced lamb or beef,
    or a mixture of the two

4 garlic cloves, crushed

10ml Roasted Masala (page 213),
    or curry powder

5ml turmeric

5ml salt, milled black pepper

2 slices bread, crumbled

60ml milk

finely grated zest and juice of 1 small lemon

1 egg

100g dried apricots, chopped

1 granny smith apple, peeled, cored
    and finely chopped

60ml sultanas

50g slivered almonds

6 lemon, orange or bay leaves

CUSTARD TOPPING

250ml milk

2 eggs

2ml salt

Heat the oven to 160°C. Butter a large casserole or 8 smaller dishes for individual servings. Heat a little butter and oil in a large saucepan and fry the onions until golden. Add the mince and fry until lightly sealed. Stir in the garlic, masala or curry powder and turmeric, then season with salt and pepper. Cover and simmer over very low heat for about 30 minutes until the meat is tender.

Mix together the crumbs, milk, lemon zest and juice, egg, apricots, apple, sultanas and almonds, and mix into the mince. Transfer the mixture to the casserole or baking dishes and pat the top nice and flat.

Roll up the lemon or bay leaves and bury them in the bobotie. Cover with foil and bake for about 30 minutes until the bobotie is firm and well cooked. Remove the casserole or baking dishes from the oven. Increase the oven heat to 200°C.

CUSTARD TOPPING Mix together the milk, eggs and salt, pour over the bobotie and bake uncovered for about 15 minutes until set and lightly browned. Serve with Yellow Rice (page 65) and Blatjang (page 161).

VENISON LOIN
WITH BACON AND HERBED APPLES

Plains game was once plentiful, providing more than enough meat for the pot. Today it's largely limited to the winter hunting months and we can get plenty of antelope like springbok, impala, kudu, blesbok and gemsbok. All would be good in this recipe, which highlights, our love of partnering meat with a sweet side-kick. Chances are the meat was bagged by professional culling and has already been hung, both of which impact positively on tenderness. There's a move away from overcooking venison, which dries out the already-lean meat.

serves 8 to 10

1,2–1,5 kg boned loin of gemsbok,
    kudu or springbok
milled black pepper
250g rindless streaky bacon
250ml Beef Stock (page 217)
125ml port

HERBED APPLES

10 granny smith apples
10 herb sprigs (thyme, rosemary,
    lavender)
juice of 1 lemon
brown sugar

Heat the oven to 180°C. Season the meat with pepper and wrap neatly in bacon. Place the meat on the rack of a roaster. Pour the beef stock into the pan. Roast uncovered until the meat is done medium-rare; about 25 to 35 minutes, depending on the thickness of the loin. Lift the meat from the rack, tent with foil and allow to rest for about 10 minutes before serving.

Place the roaster on the stovetop and boil the stock uncovered until reduced by half. Add the port and continue boiling until the gravy has reduced and thickened. Check the flavour and correct if necessary by adding salt and pepper.

HERBED APPLES Core the apples and score them round their middles; leave the skin on. Place in a baking dish. Nestle a herb sprig into each hollowed core and sprinkle with lemon juice and brown sugar. Roast at 180°C for about 30 minutes until soft.

Place the meat on a serving plate with the herbed apples alongside. Offer the gravy separately.

curries & cane fields;
sardines & spices
kwazulu-natal

THE LUSH, SUBTROPICAL GARDEN PROVINCE OF KWAZULU-NATAL IS A CULINARY RENDEZVOUS BETWEEN EAST AND WEST.

Flavours on menus here are inextricably linked with its forebears – black people who migrated from central Africa during the Iron Age, British and Scottish settlers, Mauritian immigrants who planted bananas, mangoes, lychees and pawpaws, and Indians who introduced richly spiced cuisines of their homeland. Contradictions in culinary terms – gastronomic bliss for those interested in traditional foods of a wide variety of people.

KwaZulu-Natal has been inhabited for many thousands of years. Ancient tools have been unearthed as evidence of Stone Age hunting camps, and folk who grew crops and kept herds of livestock. More recent history records that, though already inhabited by a few San and the remnants of Zimbabwe's Karanga tribe – accomplished metal workers – the area was settled early in the seventeenth century by the Nguni people who came south through Mozambique from the great lakes' region of central East Africa. They built beehive huts of branches domed with plaited grass and formed family groups, laying the foundations of the Zulu nation.

Their crops flourished in fertile soil, livestock grew fat, prolific plains game augmented their diet of amasi (curdled milk), maize meal, gourds, millet and sorghum. Sorghum also forms the base of a potent traditional beer with wide-ranging social importance in ceremonies, feasts – even in settling disputes.

The bright lights of Durban contrasts dramatically with rural KwaZulu-Natal. It's a holiday spot, an industrial force to be reckoned with, and home to a multi-national population who take pride in preserving their traditional ways of living and eating.

It is also one of Africa's principal cargo ports. Durban's natural harbor was formed some 150 million years ago when cataclysmic subterranean forces sculpted Africa's coastline. Portuguese navigators named the harbor *Rio de Natal* (river of the Nativity) or *Parve de Pescari* (the fisheries) because fish traps made from wattle fencing woven with reeds were set in the shallows by the Lala and Luthuli people.

Protected in the north by a sandspit and in the south by the high, bushy ridge known to Europeans as The Bluff and to Africans as *isi Bubulungu* (the long, bulky thing), the harbor lured seafarers and pioneering European, Indian Ocean island and Asian settlers. The motley collection of people included pirates, slave traders, merchants, shipwrecked sailors and war refugees.

There was a rich abundance of wildlife. Waters teemed with fish, waterfowl and hippos were plentiful, and trees were alive with chattering monkeys and chirping birds. Plains game and big game proliferated, including elephant – their tusks an irresistible attraction for ivory traders.

Voortrekkers came to establish their own state far from British oppression at the Cape, coinciding with the arrival of scatterlings from Shaka's efforts to build his territory. This lead to more strife as Boer and Brit fought each other for possession of the land.

ABOVE: *A Zulu woman in traditional garb patiently grinds corn for meal between two stones.*

TOP RIGHT: *A brilliantly coloured guinea fowl pecking in the grass for food.*

The province's important sugar cane industry began inauspiciously. First there was a species of wild sugar cane Zulus called mpha. Then a cargo of 'red cane' was brought to the area from the island of Mauritius. A Mauritian, Ephraim Rathbone, planted a crop, thereby launching an industry that today produces sufficient of the sweet stuff to satisfy both local demands and a lucrative export market.

In 1860 Indians came to KwaZulu-Natal under contract to work in the cane fields, creating a vital labour force and impacting on the culinary ethic of the province, and ultimately on the cuisine of South Africa. They came from varying linguistic, geographic, class and religious backgrounds, each stream remaining true to its own cooking traditions.

They brought seeds of vegetables and herbs and planted them in gardens. Key foods and spices were imported. Improvization became the mother of invention, and Indian housewives drew on local influences such as European (especially in cakes and desserts), African (pap, beans and suchlike), and even Cape Malay (bobotie, bredies and sosaties) to form a South Africanized version of Indian cuisine.

South of Durban the Agulhas current follows the continental shelf, compressing a counter-current flowing northwards. This results in the extraordinary 'sardine run' that happens in June or July most years, when migrating sardines form hundreds of vast swirling shoals, and fish are cast onto beaches in glittering heaps. Folk come from near and far to help themselves to a take-away meal. The sardines also attract predators such as sharks, dolphins, seals and seabirds. A 'bait ball' is formed when sharks and dolphins herd sardines into a tight ball, and dive into it for their own fishy feast.

In a jumble of crumpled hills and valleys north of Durban – a land previously known as Zululand or KwaZulu (home of the Zulu) – is an area of visual splendour, agricultural significance and historical importance.

Though the coastal belt is hot and humid, cool sea breezes carry rains to the high-lying hills, nourishing luxuriant vegetation, cane fields and pineapple plantations, and swelling rivers on their journey to the sea. Savannah and grasslands are interspersed by dense bush and thick

forests – perfect for wild game, now protected in private game ranches and conservation areas.

This is the heart of Maputaland, an early trader's route so richly described in H Rider Haggard's evocative writings. From here one can explore vast and varied areas encompassing diverse ecosystems – from Kosi Bay in the north to the wetlands of Lake St Lucia in the south; from the Lebombo Mountains in the west, to the fishing paradise of the Indian Ocean in the east.

The rural area of the Midlands, inland of Durban, is a world of tranquil hills and peaceful vales. The region is embraced in the west by the Drakensberg, which form a natural barrier with Lesotho. Zulus know these mountains as Ukathlamba (the barrier); Sothos call them Dilomo tsa Natal (the cliffs of Natal), while whites nicknamed them 'the mountains of the dragon' from legendary monsters which lived in the peaks.

The San, who hunted antelope on the Drakensberg's grassy foothills, crossed the mountain at what is known as the Sani Pass, leaving behind drawings in the sandstone overhangs of the sheltering cliffs as testimony of their existence.

Today cattle graze where once antelope roamed free; modern highways leading to historical guest houses have replaced dusty byways that once clattered with the sound of ox wagon wheels.

A network of rivers and patchwork of lakes and dams form the heartland of the trout fishing industry. The brown trout descends from the spawn of a couple of barrels that survived the trip from Scotland to Natal in 1890. Prosperous hatcheries now provide fish to stock other farms for fly-fishing purposes, and retail outlets for general consumption.

A gourmet's overview of KwaZulu-Natal is far removed from those who first arrived and tucked into the province's abundant fish and veldfood. Menus reflect the nuances of the cuisines of all the provinces' peoples – oriental spices, Indian Ocean island abundance and colonial conservatism.

OPPOSITE, LEFT: *A bright bowl of plump red and green chillies ready to cook up in a curry or to grind into a fresh masala.*
OPPOSITE, RIGHT: *Traditional Zulu dress is characterized by brilliantly-coloured beadwork that is worn as jewellery as well as adorning headgear and clothes.*

Necessity guided early cooks. Forever on the move, they bagged food from the veld, fished it from the sea and cooked it over the coals of a fire.

the braai

CHAPTER TWELVE

SOUTH AFRICANS LOVE NOTHING BETTER THAT a casual OUTDOOR meal. The name vleisbraai (or braaivleis) was coined at early Cape fairs and festivals. Early meats included venison and wild birds; later lamb, beef and pork were sizzling on the grid. All parts of the animal were enjoyed, including the offal – always a special treat.

Seashores are perfect places to find fishy snacks. Backdropped by crashing waves, a sea breeze and a few fisherman's tales, braaiing your catch is an appealing option.

Fuel for the fire is a hotly debated topic; many braaiers swear by coals from wood or charcoal. Winelands' braaiers consider wingerdstokke (vine stumps) superior to the Free State's dried maize cobs. Rhenosterbos of the bushveld vies in the flavour stakes with the Western Cape's rooikrantz.

Simple side dishes and salads are best. Foil-wrapped vegetables such as potatoes, onions, mushrooms, gem squash and butternut are easy to cook in the coals. Alternatively – for extra flavour and smokiness – spear them on skewers and cook on the grid.

Bread is a popular part of the menu. Top choice is potbrood (pot bread) made the way our burgher forebears did: bread dough patted into a well-buttered cast-iron potjie nestled in medium coals, with extra coals scooped onto the lid to brown the crust. For roosterkoek (grid bread) make a fairly stiff dough, shape small balls and place on a grid over medium coals. As soon as the underside is crisp, turn carefully and cook until they sound hollow when tapped. Cool, split and serve with butter. Askoek (ash bread) is cooked directly in the coals of the fire. Simply form the dough into flattish cakes the size of your palm and bake on the grid. For stokbrood (stick bread) twist dough firmly onto green sticks and hold them over the coals until crisply cooked.

It's a good idea to have everything on hand before you start to braai, with meat ready to go and side dishes (and guests) waiting; the feast should be eaten the moment it comes off the grid. When the cooking's done, pile wood on the fire and watch as the crackling blaze draws everyone into the circle of its friendly glow.

coaL-roasteD garLic

Whole heads of garlic are perfect for roasting in foil in the coals. Then simply split the cloves and squish them onto your meat or into a baked potato. If there's any garlic left over, pack it in a jar and fill with oil, and you'll have garlic-flavoured oil on hand to cook with. Store in the fridge.

serves 4

2 plump, whole heads of garlic
olive oil
salt and milled black pepper

the Longer garLic cooks, the miLDer the flavour, so aLLow a good hour of cooking over very Low coaLs for the best resuLts.

Slice off the tops of the garlic heads to expose the tips of the cloves. Pull them slightly apart and place on two sheets of heavy foil. Drizzle liberally with olive oil, season with salt and pepper and wrap securely. Nestle in coolish coals for about an hour until tender.

BRAAIED SWEETCORN

Fresh green sweetcorn (also known as mealies, corn and maize) are a favourite among all population groups, most often simply boiled and buttered, but often roasted over the embers of a fire. It's important that sweetcorn is fresh – in a perfect world this would be straight from the vegetable patch in the garden to the fire.

SERVES 6

6 sweetcorn
salt
melted butter

Remove the leaves and silk from the sweetcorn, season with salt and brush liberally with melted butter.

Braai over hot coals for 20 to 30 minutes until the kernels are smoky and delicious, brushing occasionally with more melted butter. Turn frequently to ensure even cooking.

FOILED POTATOES WITH ROOIBOS-GLAZED ONIONS

Just about any vegetable can be cooked in the coals with a protective layer of foil. A gentle prod is all you need to check when they're done, and the cooking time is forgiving, allowing you to focus on the meat instead.

SERVES 6

6 large potatoes
olive oil
salt and milled black pepper
Rooibos-glazed Onions (page 160)

Rub the potatoes with olive oil and season with salt and pepper. Wrap securely in two layers of heavy foil.

Nestle in medium-hot coals and roast for about 45 minutes until done. Unwrap the potatoes and arrange in a serving dish. Cut crosses into the tops, press open and fill with a spoonful of rooibos-glazed onions.

braaied fish with apricot glaze

West Coasters have braaied their snoek this way for many, many years; the firm, tasty flesh goes well with the tangy, fruity glaze. Any fresh linefish may be used. For added flavour, scatter fresh herbs on the coals as the fish cooks. If you prefer, cut the fish into serving portions before braaiing.

serves 8 to 10

1 whole fish, about 3kg
coarse salt
milled black pepper
vegetable oil
125ml smooth apricot jam
45ml worcestershire sauce
lemon wedges, for squeezing

Cut off the fish head and vlek open so that it hinges at the belly. Leave the skin on. Season lightly with coarse salt and set aside for 30 to 60 minutes to firm up and flavour the fish. Rinse off the salt and season the fish with a little pepper. Brush both the fish and a hinged grid with oil. Place the fish on the grid.

Mix together the jam and worcestershire sauce and liberally brush the flesh side of the fish. Close the grid and brown, flesh-side first, over hot coals. This will take about 5 to 10 minutes, depending on the heat of the coals.

Turn the fish, baste again and cook skin-side down for about 10 minutes more until cooked through. Serve with lemon wedges for squeezing.

BeRBeRe fish
with avocado and melon salad

Ethiopian berbere (or berbiri) means 'hot sauce', named after the Berbers, nomads of North Africa. Berbere paste is perfect to perk up fresh, whole fish cooked over the coals. Fish in the lightweight division – 500g to 750g – are best, as the heat penetrates quickly to the bone.

serves 4

4 whole fish, 500g–750g each
salt and milled black pepper
mint sprigs and fennel fronds
60ml Berbere Paste (page 215)
olive oil

AVOCADO AND MELON SALAD

1 avocado
½ small sweet melon (spanspek)
60ml chopped coriander
30ml roughly chopped mint leaves
45ml olive oil
juice of 2 limes
salt and milled black pepper

Scale and gut the fish, make a few deep slashes in the sides and season with salt and pepper. Tuck mint sprigs and fennel fronds into the body cavities. Smear berbere paste all over and rub in with your hands. Place in a dish and drizzle with olive oil. Set aside for a couple of hours in a cool spot (or in the fridge).

AVOCADO AND MELON SALAD Peel and stone the avocado and cut into small cubes. Toss into a bowl. Skin and pip the melon and cut into small cubes. Add to the avocado with the coriander and mint. Pour over the olive oil and flavour with lime juice, salt and pepper. Toss everything together.

Braai the fish over medium-hot coals for about 25 minutes until cooked through, turning frequently. Serve one per person with avocado and melon salad on the side.

Jawaharlal Nehru, first prime minister of India, was so fond of tandoori chicken that he insisted that it was served at state banquets.

tandoori chicken with charred pineapple

This spicy, succulent chicken originated in India, a country that knows what's what in the flavour stakes. It's usually cooked over very high heat in a tandoor – a cylindrical clay oven fired by charcoal – which results in a seductively crisp skin. Braaiing over the coals is the next best thing, but as the marinade has a tendency to burn, it's preferable to brush it off beforehand.

serves 4

1 chicken
salt and milled black pepper
10ml paprika
250ml plain yoghurt
10ml Green Masala (page 213)
5ml turmeric
vegetable oil
1 pineapple, skinned and
  sliced

Butterfly the chicken by cutting through the backbone so it hinges open. Press flat, wash well and pat dry. Place in a non-metal dish and season with salt, pepper and paprika.

Mix together the yoghurt, masala and turmeric. Pour over the chicken and marinate in the fridge for at least 5 hours – overnight is even better. Lift the chicken from the marinade and brush it off. Drizzle over a little oil and rub it in.

Braai the chicken over medium-hot coals, turning occasionally, until done. This should take about 50 minutes depending on the heat of the coals and the size of the bird. Towards the end of the cooking time, roast the pineapple on the grid until well browned and deliciously tender.

Place the chicken on a warm plate and garnish with pineapple.

spiced minced meat
on skewers is a famous
indian dish dating
from moghul emperors
who invaded india
in past centuries.

skilpadjies

Lamb's liver wrapped in netvet (caul fat) – also known as muise, vlermuise and tortoises – are an old Cape delicacy. They're named after tortoises which roam free and which were made into soup in the 'bad old days'. Some cooks prefer to mince or chop the liver and mix it with breadcrumbs and chopped onion. A similar favourite among black communities is chopped liver mixed with meat and stuffed into the large intestine of the animal before being cooked.

serves 4 to 6

500g lamb's liver
salt and milled black pepper
1 lamb caul (netvet)
lemon wedges, for squeezing

Rinse the liver in cold water and pull off the membrane. Cut into chunks and season lightly with salt and pepper. Spread the caul on a board, cut into pieces and wrap the pieces of liver. Secure with toothpicks so the parcels don't unravel as they cook.

Braai the skilpadjies quickly on both sides over high heat – they should still be pink in the centre. Serve as they come off the grid with lemon wedges for squeezing.

keema seekh kebabs

Choose mince that's slightly fatty for these kebabs (which makes them more succulent) and impale the meatballs on steel squared Indian skewers (seekhs) if you have them. To serve as snacks, fry in hot oil until well browned and almost cooked through. Serve with Dhai (page 154) to dip them in.

serves 6 to 8

500g minced lamb, beef or ostrich
5ml Green Masala (page 213)
2ml ground cumin
2ml ground coriander
5ml salt
2ml turmeric
30ml chopped coriander
1 onion, very finely chopped

Mix all the ingredients together and form the mixture into balls. Thread onto skewers. Braai over hot coals for about 8 minutes, turning frequently so they brown and cook evenly.

BOEREWORS

Making this world-famous 'farmer's sausage' is a satisfying (though time-consuming) task; one you won't want to do on the day of the braai. For the best flavour and succulence, boerewors should mature for a few days in the fridge before cooking. It may be frozen for three months.

makes 3,5kg

2kg beef from the forequarter

1kg fatty pork (neck, shoulder or belly)

45ml coriander seeds

5ml whole cloves

30ml salt

15ml milled black pepper

2ml grated nutmeg

10ml ground allspice

10ml brown sugar

125ml dry red wine or red wine vinegar

90g thick sausage casings, soaked
  in water

Pap with Spinach (page 62), to serve

Trim the beef and pork of fat, sinews and other extraneous bits and pieces. Cut into long, narrow strips about 3cm in diameter and freeze for about 30 minutes. This makes it easier to mince.

For a nice rough texture, mince through a coarse mincer. Feed the meat through with little help from the tamper. Finish by mincing a piece of bread to remove the last vestiges of meat from the mincer.

Roast the coriander and cloves in a dry frying pan, tossing them about until browned and aromatic. Don't let them burn! Grind with a pestle and mortar, then sift to remove the husks. Mix in the salt, pepper, nutmeg, allspice and brown sugar. Sprinkle over the mince with the wine or vinegar. Mix everything together.

Drain the sausage casings. Place one end over the filling horn and push on, leaving a 10cm length hanging down. Tie a knot in this. Feed the sausage mixture into the mincer a little at a time, while securing the casing with gentle pressure on the horn to control the unrolling of the casing. Don't pack the casing too full, or the boerewors will burst while cooking. And try to avoid air bubbles. Remove the sausage – still attached to the horn – from the machine. Push any remaining mixture into the casing and tie a knot in the end.

Braai the boerewors quickly over hot coals. The skin should be crisp and the middle slightly pink. Serve immediately with pap and spinach.

BOEREWORS IS ATTRIBUTED TO EARLY GERMAN SETTLERS WHO KNEW ALL THERE WAS TO KNOW ABOUT SAUSAGE-MAKING.

Lamb sosaties

The name 'sosatie' comes from the Malay words saté (spiced sauce) and sésate (skewered meat). The meat can be skewered on any handy branches: quince trees are favoured in the Karoo, while twigs of red ivory and magic guarri trees are popular in the bushveld. Like many spiced, semi-preserved dishes, sosaties were once padkos (road food) for ox wagon and horse-drawn carriage journeys. Any type of meat will do, including beef, ostrich and pork. Interspersing the meat with fat makes it more succulent, though some braaiers prefer to leave it out. Bacon is fine, but slivers of fat from around sheep's kidneys is best, as it's finer and melts while cooking.

makes about 16

1 leg of lamb (2kg–2,5kg)
125g dried or semi-dried apricots
sheeps' fat, cut into fine slivers, or pieces
    of rindless streaky bacon (optional)

MARINADE
2 onions, quartered
125ml white wine vinegar
375ml dry red wine
12 lemon leaves, bruised
4 thin slices peeled green ginger
15ml brown sugar
45ml curry powder
15ml ground coriander
5ml ground allspice
2ml ground cinnamon
2ml ground cumin
10ml salt
1ml ground cardamom
milled black pepper

Bone, trim and cube the lamb. Place in a dish. Combine the marinade ingredients in a medium saucepan, cover and simmer for 5 minutes. Cool, then pour over the meat, turning to coat it well. Cover and refrigerate for 3 to 5 days for the best flavour, turning the meat in the marinade once or twice a day.

Place the dried apricots in a small bowl, pour over boiling water, and leave to plump for an hour or two. Semi-dried apricots don't require any soaking.

Thread the meat, fat or bacon, apricots and slices of onion (from the marinade) onto skewers. Braai over hot coals, basting with the remaining marinade, for 10 to 15 minutes. The lamb should still be pink and moist in the centre.

taverns in old cape town were known as 'sosatie and rice houses' in honour of these succulent kebabs, which are one of the country's all-time favourite braai treats.

BRITAIN CHAMPIONED THE PARTNERSHIP OF ROAST LAMB AND MINT SAUCE. A NATURAL AFRICAN FUSION MOVES THINGS UP A NOTCH BY SPICING UP THE MEAT AND SERVING IT WITH MINT- AND CORIANDER-FLAVOURED YOGHURT.

malay-spiced lamb chops

There's nothing nicer than plump lamb chops marinated in an exotic Cape Malay flavour mix and crisped over the coals. Serve 1 to 2 chops per person, depending on size.

serves 6

6–12 lamb chump or loin chops
salt and milled black pepper
4 garlic cloves
small knob green ginger, peeled
1 red or green chilli, sliced and seeded
125ml olive or vegetable oil
60ml chutney
30ml lemon juice
10ml ground coriander

Trim the chops, season with salt and pepper and place in a non-metal dish.

Crush the garlic, ginger and chilli with a pestle and mortar. Mix in the oil, chutney, lemon juice and coriander. Pour over the chops and turn to coat well with the marinade. Cover and set aside for about 4 hours. Turn occasionally to flavour evenly.

Braai the chops over medium-low heat for about 5 minutes on each side until done. They should be crisp on the surface and pink within.

rack of lamb with herbed dhai

Ethiopian berbere paste defines many spiced-up dishes in that country, and perks up this lamb dish no end. Add a cooling yoghurt side-kick and you have a dish that's bliss in any language!

serves 2 to 3

1 rack of lamb (5–6 chops; about 500g)
olive oil
Berbere Paste (page 215)
salt and milled black pepper
rosemary sprigs

HERBED DHAI
10g coriander leaves
10g mint leaves
125ml plain yoghurt

Brush the lamb with olive oil, rub with berbere paste, and season with salt and pepper. Pack rosemary sprigs between the chops.

HERBED DHAI Chop the coriander and mint. Stir in the yoghurt and season with salt and pepper. Scoop into a bowl. Cover and chill until serving time.

Braai the lamb over hot coals until well browned and crusty. Raise the grid from the heat and continue to cook over lower heat until done to your liking – about 25 minutes for meat that's still tinged with pink. Allow the meat to rest for about 10 minutes before serving, with herbed dhai on the side.

masala-crusted beef fillet with north african citrus glaze

Like most spicings, masalas are available ready-made, but home-made blends are much fresher and more piquantly spiced. Perfect for adding a bit of drama to beef fillet.

serves 6 to 8

1,5–2kg whole beef fillet
olive oil
Roasted Masala (page 213)
salt and milled black pepper

NORTH AFRICAN
    CITRUS GLAZE
15ml curmin seeds
500ml orange juice
finely grated zest and juice
    of 1 lemon
60ml honey

Trim the fillet and place in a dish. Rub well with olive oil. Sprinkle over a little roasted masala and press well into the surface. Set aside at room temperature for 3 to 4 hours (or overnight in the fridge), turning occasionally. Bring the meat to room temperature before braaiing.

When your coals are hot, brown the fillet well on all sides. Continue braaiing, rolling the meat so it cooks evenly. It will be medium-rare in about 20 minutes. Allow a little longer if you prefer well-done meat; remove the fillet from the grid sooner for rare beef.

Allow the steak to rest for at least 10 minutes before carving into thickish slices. Season with salt and pepper. Serve with North African citrus glaze.

NORTH AFRICAN CITRUS GLAZE Roast the cumin in a dry frying pan. Pound to a paste with a pestle and mortar. Tip into a medium saucepan. Add the orange juice, lemon zest and juice, and honey. Boil uncovered, stirring occasionally, until reduced by two-thirds and nicely thickened.

windmills & wheat fields; sunflowers & sheep

the free state

13

TWO RIVERS FORM THE BOUNDARIES OF THIS GENTLY UNDULATING PRAIRIELAND — THE ORANGE IN THE SOUTH; THE VAAL IN THE NORTH. IN BETWEEN ARE FARMS, RURAL TOWNS AND VILLAGES, AND, TO BREAK THE MONOTONY OF THE HORIZON AS YOU HURTLE ALONG THE HIGHWAY BETWEEN THE CAPE AND GAUTENG, OCEANS OF MAIZE AND WHEAT FIELDS, FLOCKS OF FAT, CONTENTED SHEEP, AND WINDMILLS STANDING STARK AGAINST A BRILLIANT SKY.

In the eastern highlands savannah sweeps on to meet the mighty Drakensberg, 'dragon mountains', where the Free State, KwaZulu-Natal and the kingdom of Lesotho, home of the Basotho, meet atop the Mont-aux-Sources. Five rivers rise in the 'mountain of beginnings', including those that embrace the Free State.

The many name-changes of this province echo the path of its human and political history. In sandstone caves in the eastern hills the San left stone implements, bone artefacts, and rock art. Ancient images of these prehistoric artists show that they hunted plains game like springbok, blesbok, hartebeest, gnu (wildebeest) and quagga. Other clans like the Leghoja, Basotho, Barolong, Korana and Griqua followed the San to the hunting grounds.

The mighty Orange River was called !Gariep (great river) by the Khoikhoi; the area beyond was Transgariep. In 1779 Colonel Robert Gordon, explorer and commander of the Dutch East India Company, renamed it in honour of the Prince of Orange; the area beyond the river became Transorangia.

Early in the nineteenth century white hunters came to this game-rich plateau. When word of the lush soil reached the Cape, trek-farmers, in the grip of a prolonged drought in southern farmlands, arrived in search of good grazing. The Voortrekkers followed the farmers, and the name-changing continued. The governor of the Cape Colony later claimed the province for Britain, and named it the Orange River Sovereignty. In 1854 the Republic of the Orange Free State was proclaimed by the boers. During the Anglo-Boer War it was renamed the Orange River Colony. In 1910 it became the Orange Free State, one of the four provinces of the Union of South Africa. After the general elections in 1994, it was finally named Free State.

Though gold and uranium are mined here, the rich soil remains the Free State's most enduring claim to prosperity. Because wheat grows so well, it's known as the 'bread basket' of South Africa. Bread also spawned the naming of the town of Bethlehem in the foothills of the Maluti Mountains, for Christ's birthplace means 'house of bread'. The river running through the valley was named the Jordan.

The Free State also grows groundnuts, sunflowers, potatoes, onions, peas, beans and pumpkins, and more asparagus than anywhere in the country. Wild asparagus was well known to early Cape colonists, who gathered the tender sprouts and nicknamed it cat briar. It grew well in Jan van Riebeeck's vegetable garden, and was enjoyed by passing seamen. Many years later, at a Roman Catholic monastery in Harrismith at the foothills of the Platberg in the eastern Free State, a horticulturalist cultivated wild asparagus. Seeds were later imported from America. Full-scale farming commenced in the 1950s, and today fresh and tinned asparagus is produced for the home and export markets.

Pretty Ficksburg, on the banks of the Caledon River (which the Basotho call the Mohokare, or 'willow trees' after the willows which line its banks), bordering Lesotho, is the hub of the cherry industry. Ripe, luscious berries and by-products, such as cherry brandy and cherry liqueur, are enjoyed by cherry-lovers from far and near, and cherry dishes are created by cooks at local restaurants and guest houses.

Bloemfontein, 'city of roses', started as a humble stock farm. The farmer's wife planted a flower garden beside a spring which blacks called Mangaung (place of leopards). The spring was subsequently named Bloem Fonteyn (flower fountain) and the mud-brick farmhouse was remodelled into a grand residence which was home to the first three presidents of the Republic of the Orange Free State.

BELOW: *A typical Free State scene of a farmer's barn and windmill backdropped by a moody sky.*

Life in the free state is dominated by the changing seasons which, in turn, influence the province's livelihood of small- and large-scale farming.

Vrystaters have a reputation for generous, warm-hearted hospitality. They care little for changing food fashions, preferring hearty potfuls of the homely stuff that feeds body and soul in equal measure. Simple guest houses and inns at wayside farms entice travellers to take time out at a slower pace, and to explore menus filled with comfort food. Buffets groan with roasts and casseroles like curried tripe, bobotie, oxtail, and tongue in mustard sauce, and pies of lamb, venison and chicken. Blesbok, indigenous to the region, draped with bacon and roasted to perfection, often has pride of place.

Home cooks proudly recreate recipes passed down from mother to daughter. Farmers are skilled at the art of sizzling meat over the embers of maize husks. Their wives prepare traditional salads and delicious home-grown, home-bottled chutneys, relishes and jams to accompany the braai, as well as to stock the shelves of home-industry shops and the trestle tables at fêtes and bazaars.

Life in the Free State is dominated by the changing seasons, which in turn influence the province's livelihood – large- and small-scale farming. The clear blue skies of spring give way to thunderclouds and darkening skies of summer. When rains have fallen and the sun breaks through, rainbows arch the horizons. Autumn landscapes are tinged with warm russets and reds. Winter chills the central and southern flatlands and offers its own visual magic in the highlands and Lesotho – glorious snow-capped mountains, only to melt again as the ancient cycle of seasons begins once more.

OPPOSITE, TOP: *Mealies are an important Free State crop, and should be eaten as soon as possible after they have been picked.*
OPPOSITE, BELOW: *Pink and white cosmos flowers grow wild in the Golden Gate National Park.*
RIGHT: *A farmer proudly displays a plump pumpkin ready to be cooked up into a simple and nourishing meal for the family.*

serving a variety of sambals is the perfect way to add a bit of drama to the plainest meal by adding flavour and texture and a splash of colour.

sambals

CHAPTER FOURTEEN

Before indian indentured labourers arrived in kwazulu-natal and Malay slaves were brought from the East, local dishes emulated the plain, solid fare of Holland and Germany.

Slaves became the cooks of early colonists and Indians brought with them their favourite spices, so an exciting patina of Oriental brilliance was quickly added to local menus, not least in the introduction of sambals, atjars and pickles.

Cool sambals were served with hot dishes; blander dishes were offered with chilli-hot ones. Indian raitas (spiced yoghurt) and crunchy kachoomers (based on chopped or sliced onion) found favour too.
Fresh coriander and mint were dominant herbs; chilli, cumin and dried coriander the favourite spices.

Atjar is a generic name for a variety of pickles. Some were imported; others freshly prepared or purchased at markets and shops specializing in Oriental and Eastern fare. Chutneys were made from onions, tomatoes, apples, coconut and dates. Indian-style pickled mangoes, lemons, limes, dried fruit and vegetables provide additional tongue-tingling heat to perk up anything from curries to roasted and braaied meat and fish.

BOTTLING TIPS
Some of the recipes in this chapter require bottling in sterilized jars. Here's how to do it:
- Wash jars in hot, sudsy water. Rinse well and drain.
- Place jars open-side up on a baking tray, with lids alongside and sterilize in the oven for about 20 minutes at 110°C. Bottles must be hot and dry when filled.
- Always use a large saucepan to prevent the mixture from boiling over. Use only stainless steel saucepans.
- Tilt jars to prevent air bubbles, and fill to the brim. If you're using metal tops, cover first with melted wax or waxed paper. Seal with the lid while still hot; label with contents and date.
- Store in a dry, cool, dark place for up to six months. Keep refrigerated once opened.

DHAI

This Malay yoghurt side dish is perfect with spicy meat dishes such as curries and breyanis.

makes 250mL

250ml thick, plain yoghurt

salt and milled black pepper

1 garlic clove, crushed

½ green chilli, sliced, seeded and very finely chopped

1ml ground cumin

juice of ½ lemon

60ml chopped coriander

Mix the ingredients together in a bowl, cover and chill.

APPLE-MINT RELISH

This tangy Indian relish is quick to whip up and equally delicious with a curry or with braaied lamb chops.

makes 250mL

2 large granny smith apples

250ml lightly packed mint leaves

2ml salt

1 garlic clove

2ml Green Masala (page 213)

juice of ½ lemon

Peel, core and slice the apples. Place all the ingredients in a food processor and whizz to a thick purée. Cover and chill before serving.

CUCUMBER RAITA

This Indian raita has a base of yoghurt and lots of spice.

makes 250mL

½ English cucumber

2ml Green Masala (page 213)

125ml chopped coriander

15ml lemon juice

250ml thick, plain yoghurt

salt

Slice the cucumber into quarters lengthwise, then seed and cut into small cubes. Mix together the masala, coriander, lemon juice and yoghurt in a bowl, and season with salt. Stir in the cucumber and chill for an hour or two before serving.

CORIANDER AND MINT CHUTNEY

Coriander and mint feature prominently in Indian recipes, and team up here in a wonderful fresh chutney.

makes about 250mL

30g coriander

20g mint leaves

5ml Green Masala (page 213)

2ml ground cumin

30ml lemon juice

Chop the coriander and mint. Stir in the masala, cumin and lemon juice. Scoop into a bowl, cover and chill before serving.

there's no need to
serve sambals only with
curries and other spicy
dishes; they also make
good side servings for
roast meat.

quince sambal

Quinces are a wonderful old-fashioned fruit. In the olden days they were preserved by salting, drying and packing in wickerwork containers. They were also made into this Malay sambal, which is great with curry and roast beef or lamb. It's a good idea to make it a day or two ahead for the fruit to soften and the flavours to mingle.

makes about 250ml

1 quince
salt
5–6 spring onions, finely sliced
1 garlic clove, crushed
1 red chilli, sliced and seeded
30ml sugar
juice of 2 lemons

Peel, quarter and core the quince, and slice into fine slivers. Pile into a bowl, sprinkle with salt and set aside for an hour or two. Rinse with cold water, drain well, and dry thoroughly. Tip into a bowl, mix in the remaining ingredients, cover and chill.

kumquat pickle

This spicy preserve is perfect with venison and roasted or braaied red meats like beef, lamb or ostrich. It improves with keeping and may be stored in the fridge for six months.

makes 4 x 300ml jars

1kg ripe kumquats
375ml wine or malt vinegar
600g sugar
20 black peppercorns
20 whole cloves
2 star anise
5ml ground allspice
5ml ground cinnamon

Wash and destalk the kumquats. Cut in half and remove the pips. Combine the remaining ingredients in a medium saucepan. Bring to the boil, stirring constantly until the sugar dissolves. Cover and simmer over very low heat for about 10 minutes.

Add the kumquats to the syrup, cover and simmer for about 10 minutes until softened. The cooking time depends on how ripe the fruit was at the start. Remove the lid and simmer uncovered for about 20 minutes more until the syrup thickens slightly and the fruit is perfectly tender. Stir occasionally.

Bottle the kumquat pickle in hot, sterilized jars while still hot. Store in the fridge.

west african banana chutney

Bananas and plantains, grown in southern Africa since the earliest times, are served fresh, baked, stewed, and made into puddings and salads. This chutney is particularly good with braaied fish or chicken.

serves 4 to 6

4 nearly-ripe bananas

100g brown sugar

250ml white wine vinegar

1 chilli, sliced (discard seeds for a milder flavour)

2 cardamom pods, lightly crushed

2ml cumin seeds

1 bay leaf

Peel the bananas and slice thickly. Combine the remaining ingredients in a medium saucepan. Bring to the boil, stirring until the sugar dissolves. Cover and simmer for about 3 minutes for the flavours to infuse.

Add the bananas and boil uncovered just until the fruit is soft and the syrup has thickened a little. Cooking time depends on the ripeness of the bananas; anything from 1 to 3 minutes should do it.

Serve within an hour or so of preparation, as the banana discolours quite quickly.

kumquat pickle has a natural affinity with venison, but is also great with any braaied meat.

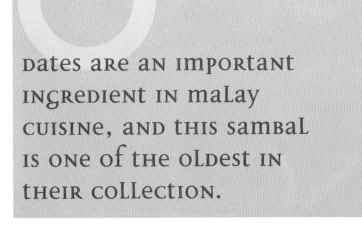

date
AND ONION sambaL

This sambal is best served on the day it's made, as the dates tend to plump up in the syrup and lose their texture.

serves 4 to 6

1 onion, finely sliced
200g fresh dates
1 green or red chilli, finely sliced and seeded
125ml cider or wine vinegar
10ml brown sugar

Place the onion in a bowl and pour over plenty of boiling water. Set aside for 5 minutes to soften, then drain well.

Stone and quarter the dates and toss in a small bowl with the onion and chilli. Mix together the vinegar and sugar, stirring until the sugar dissolves and pour over. Serve within a couple of hours of preparation.

DATES ARE AN IMPORTANT INGREDIENT IN maLay CUISINE, AND THIS SAMBAL IS ONE OF THE OLDEST IN THEIR COLLECTION.

BReaD
aND ButteR PicKLe

History sends us mixed messages about the origins of this pickle, though the strange name suggests that it could have been Britain. It's delicious with smoked fish as well as on a cheese platter. It's worth making a good amount at one go, as it keeps well.

makes 4 x 500mL jars

2 English cucumbers (about 850g)

300ml water

60ml salt

2 onions, finely sliced

1 red pepper, seeded and finely sliced

200g sugar

250ml red wine vinegar

5ml mustard seeds

5ml celery seeds

4 whole cloves

Wash the cucumbers, slice finely and place in a large bowl. Heat the water in a small saucepan, add the salt and stir until dissolved. Cool to room temperature, then pour over the cucumber. Place a plate on top to weigh the cucumber down. Place a plastic bag filled with ice blocks on top; this will keep the cucumber nice and crisp. Chill in the fridge for 3 hours.

Tip the cucumber into a colander and rinse under running water. Tip into a bowl and mix in the onions and red pepper.

Combine the sugar, vinegar, mustard seeds, celery seeds and cloves in a medium saucepan. Bring to the boil, stirring until the sugar dissolves. Pour over the vegetables. Pack into hot, sterilized jars, filling them to the brim. Seal and store in a cool, dark cupboard. Once opened, store in the fridge.

CHILLI JAM

This fiery 'jam' will perk up anything from a braaied chop to a baked potato. Don't make chilli jam with small chillies – it will drive you insane!

serves 8

200g large, fat red or green chillies
200g onions, finely sliced
200g sugar
125ml water
2ml salt
30ml lemon juice

Slice the chillies and discard the seeds if you wish; this makes the jam less hot. Place in a medium saucepan with the onions, sugar, water, salt and lemon juice. Bring slowly to the boil, stirring until the sugar dissolves. Boil uncovered for about 10 minutes until the syrup thickens. Allow to cool. Store in sterilized jars in the fridge.

ROOIBOS IS A flAVOUR YOU EITHER LOVE OR HATE, SO YOU'RE WELCOME TO SUBSTITUTE YOUR FAVOURITE HERBAL TEA IN THIS RECIPE.

ROOIBOS-GLAZED ONIONS

The only place in the world where rooibos (red bush) grows is along the Olifants River and high in the Cederberg in the Western Cape where its twigs and leaves are dried and made into tea. Mountain folk had probably been drinking it for a very long time, but the first recorded reference to rooibos was in 1790 by a botanist named Thuneberg. It's an acquired taste (one early traveller likened it to 'clippings from a privet hedge').

serves 8

500ml water
60ml sugar
finely grated zest of ½ orange
8 rooibos teabags
2 onions, finely sliced
salt and milled black pepper

Bring the water to the boil in a medium saucepan. Stir in the sugar and orange zest, then add the teabags. Cover and simmer for about 15 minutes for the flavours to infuse. Strain into a clean saucepan and discard the teabags and orange zest.

Add the onions, season with salt and pepper and cook uncovered for about 15 minutes until the liquid has almost disappeared and the onions are nicely glazed. Stir occasionally. Serve hot.

bLatjang

Before we made chutneys from apricots, dates, quinces and raisins, blatjang was imported from Java, made from pounded, sun-dried prawns. The name comes from one of the constituents of the Javanese sambal blachang. Early food writer C Louis Leipoldt described it as being 'bitingly spicy, pungently aromatic, moderately smooth and a very intimate association of the ingredients'. There's nothing quite like blatjang to add zest to curries.

makes about 1,2 Litres

250g dried apricots
250g seedless raisins
3 litres red wine vinegar
4 onions, finely chopped
4 garlic cloves, finely chopped
500g brown sugar
200g flaked almonds
30ml salt
45ml ground ginger
30ml ground coriander
30ml mustard seeds
10ml chilli powder

Chop the apricots and place in a large saucepan with the raisins and vinegar. Soak overnight to plump the fruit. Alternatively – if time is tight – cover, bring to the boil and set aside for 2 hours.

Add the remaining ingredients and cook uncovered over medium heat. Stir occasionally at first, then constantly towards the end of the cooking time, until the chutney has reduced to about one-third and is beautifully thick. It should take 1½ to 2 hours.

Pour the chutney into hot, sterilized jars and seal. Store in a cool, dark cupboard. Refrigerate once opened.

marula fruit, mopane worms, trout farms & tea

gauteng, mpumalanga, north west & limpopo

15

the northern regions of southern africa are a treasure trove of unusual edibles — bliss for inquisitive gourmets.

Here you will discover delicacies as diverse as marula fruit and mopane worms, as elusive as wild game and as prolific as subtropical fruit. Tea estates flourish; trout grow fat in streams and dams; wild mushrooms grow in lush forests; nuts ripen in tranquil groves.

This diverse region stretches from the urban sprawl of Gauteng through hills and vales of the Eastern Highlands to the splendour of Mpumalanga, past rugged escarpments and majestic mountains of the high-lying plateaux, to the sparse bushveld and savannahs of the Lowveld – big game country – and the North West Province and Limpopo.

Johannesburg, 'city of gold', and Pretoria, 'jacaranda city', are springboards for exploring these northern and eastern regions. Though the concrete jungles aren't as picturesque as coastal villages or country escapes, the variety of eateries more than compensates for the lack of charm. Restaurants cater for the full spectrum of pockets and preferences; haute cuisine rubs shoulders with homely fare, and every type of ethnic cuisine imaginable, while food-to-go stalls create business opportunities for informal entrepreneurs on city streets.

Tranquil places and open spaces are an easy drive from Gauteng, like the majestic Magaliesberge and North West Province (previously called Bophuthatswana), and KwaNdebele ('home of the Ndebele') northeast of Pretoria which provides a fascinating glimpse of the history, culture, tradition and cuisine of this artistic tribe and their brilliantly painted houses.

Mpumalanga, a world of gentle country pursuits, once echoed with the clattering ox wagons of Voortrekkers, rang with sounds of battle during the Anglo-Boer War, witnessed the triumph (and ultimate demise) of slave traders, pioneering gold-diggers, raiding bandits, fortune seekers and ivory hunters. Wild, wonderful, desperate times; gone, though not forgotten, as relics displayed in small museums remain to remind us, while tales of those early days are told round crackling bushveld fires.

Tourists relax at luxurious guest houses. Wayside tea rooms, pubs and restaurants prepare local produce like trout that have been farmed in Mpumalanga since the mid-1950s. Travellers through this pretty part of the country are assured of a wide range of feasts prepared from fresh and smoked trout, including salads, omelettes, bisques, pâtés and crusty pies.

Nelspruit and nearby White River are the centre of a vast farming region that produces citrus, pecans and macadamia nuts, and subtropical fruit such as lychees, bananas, mangoes and avocados.

Bustling Tzaneen boasts large-scale tea estates which have sister farms in Limpopo and KwaZulu-Natal, where the industry started in 1850. Rolling hills are shrouded with manicured tea bushes. Pluckers nip off the topmost leaves, toss them into baskets, and carry their fragrant load to the factory for processing. There leaves are 'withered' in troughs of warm air, minced through rollers, fermented (oxidized), dried, cleaned and graded.

Due to widespread malaria, game-rich eastern areas were largely uninhabited until the late 1800s, though settlement burgeoned after the disease had been controlled. Animal tracks soon became Voortrekker wagon trails, then even later were turned into tortuous coach routes used by transport riders carrying supplies from the coast to the eastern Transvaal goldfields, and to early farming settlements further afield.

Men took their guns with them to this treasure-house of wildlife and hunters killed for the pot as well as for pleasure and profit. Inspired by statesman Paul Kruger, spearheaded by conservationists, and implemented by the Transvaal Volksraad, the killing of elephants was curtailed in 1850, hunters were forbidden to shoot more game than they could consume, and pit-traps and snares were outlawed. Game was further protected when closed seasons were declared, allowing them to breed undisturbed for future generations to enjoy.

ABOVE LEFT: *Sunflowers grow well in the sandy soil of the North West Province and brighten the landscape for motorists as they drive by.*
ABOVE RIGHT: *Woodwork and tablecloths are offered for sale to passers-by at roadside markets.*

THE TOURIST MARKET IS IMPORTANT TO LOCALS, WHOSE SKILLS IN CRAFTING BEAUTIFUL WOODWORK ARE WORLD-RENOWNED.

vegetables
and fruit are
displayed at
roadside markets
for passers-by to
snaffle up for
a quick snack.

Wildlife sanctuaries like the Kruger National Park were created in the rich savannahs that sweep down from the great lakes of central Africa, across Zimbabwe, through Mpumalanga to Swaziland and KwaZulu-Natal, areas which now sport the largest concentration of game reserves on the continent.

In a corner of Limpopo Province bordering Zimbabwe is a mysterious place of unspoilt beauty steeped in tradition. The land previously known as Venda offers simple foods enhanced by fascinating folklore. The VhaVenda people – one of Africa's oldest tribes – have dwelled here for centuries after they followed the beat of the domba drum and crossed the mighty Limpopo River in search of sanctuary and a place to call home.

In clustered villages life goes on much the way it has done for countless years. But, like the passage of many ancient civilizations, modern life is making inroads, and time-honoured traditions are falling into disuse. Soon they will fade from memory. Nowadays maize meal is purchased in packets and women seldom grind their own meal for mukonde (King's porridge), patiently stirring it over open cooking fires, and ladling layers onto wooden plates, to be peeled off one by one.

Southern soil is lush enough for maize, coffee and tea, as well as vegetables and subtropical fruit, which is offered for sale at raggle-taggle roadside markets. In arid northern parts you'll fine sparse mopane-scrub, home to mopane worms. These pleasantly chewy delicacies are roasted over open fires, or dried and reconstituted by 'frying' in salted water. Sadly, they're becoming scarcer. Some blame escalating farming in the low-lying places mopane worms love best; others claim the supply has been stripped to its present low levels.

Mighty baobabs, one of the largest known trees in the world which live for about a thousand years, dominate the landscape by their sheer bulk (stems average seven metres in diameter). They seem to have been planted upside down, branches like roots reaching to the sky, while deep underground is another tangle which could be the original branches.

Baobabs are useful trees; the fibrous wood is macerated into rope and paper, pollen is used for glue, while leaves are cooked and served as a vegetable. Acidic seeds are ground and roasted to make 'coffee'. Fruit is pounded into flour, mixed with milk and prepared as porridge. Fruit pods contain tartaric acid, which is why the tree is sometimes called the cream of tartar tree.

Marula fruit holds a special place in the scheme of things. In February and March ripe, golden fruit falls to earth and starts fermenting – and impromptu parties happen under every tree. Marula fruit finds its way into meat stews and vegetable dishes, and makes delicious beer that is clear, sparkling and slightly aromatic.

Superstition guides the hand of the brewer: fruit is cut with a knife made from wood or the bone of goats, sheep or antelope, and a little of the brew is always set aside as an offering to appease the spirits. More appealing to Western palates is marula jelly, a perfect side dish for the variety of venison dishes which are a speciality in these northern regions of South Africa.

When next the lure of the open road beckons, head north along untravelled paths, explore places where a sense of calm still reigns, and enjoy food grown in the rich soil of a bountiful region.

OPPOSITE, TOP: *Simple rural farmhouse on the roadside in the North West Province.*
OPPOSITE, BOTTOM LEFT: *Zebra grazing peacefully in one of the many private game reserves in the area.*
OPPOSITE, BOTTOM RIGHT: *Open-air shop displaying fresh wares plucked from small-scale farms.*

SUN - RIPENED FRUIT IS THE PERFECT WAY TO END A MEAL, AFRICAN - STYLE. DISPLAY IT SIMPLY, AS IT'S DONE HERE AT GOLD RESTAURANT IN THE HEART OF CAPE TOWN.

sweetmeats & PUDDINGS

CHAPTER SIXTEEN

AFTER-DINNER SWEET TREATS HARK BACK TO COUNTRY KITCHENS AND FAMILY DINNERS — recipes that pay homage to folk for whom the sweetest pleasures are simple ones.

Puddings are not a traditional part of the African diet; they only came into vogue after Africa was colonized. Fruit from the veld such as kei-apples, quinces, wild medlars, sour plums and wild oranges satisfied those with a passion for sweet things.

Coastal dwellers gathered wild figs that grow in sand dunes, including Hottentot figs which have large yellow flowers and juicy fruit, and sour figs which make delicious jam. In the north you will find marula (which also makes a heady liqueur) and baobab fruit — large, spongy and floury, with a pleasant, acidic taste.

Later fruit was made into fruit salads, flavoured with ginger, cinnamon, nutmeg, rose water, lemon juice and naartjie (tangerine) peel. Some cooks added a dash of wine, brandy or rum as well.

For a sugar fix during long journeys, Eastern-style mebos was prepared from sun-dried, salted apricots, and plat perskes (flat peaches) which were mashed, dried and rolled or folded.

When Indians came to work on KwaZulu-Natal cane fields they introduced tropical fruits like mangoes, pawpaws, guavas and loquats to our fruit bowls, and turned them into tangy chutneys and pickles to accompany spicy dishes.

Two alien fruits were introduced during the Anglo-Boer War that began in 1899 and ended in 1902: brambleberries sprung from seeds brought from England in fodder for cavalry horses in the KwaZulu-Natal Midlands, while in the Northern Cape soldiers munched on dates from their ration packs from home, and pressed the stones into river banks, which grew into majestic date palms.

The variety of milk puddings in our repertoire reflect our Dutch and Anglo-Saxon roots, though many recipes have acquired Eastern nuances, thanks to Cape Malay cooks who added spicings to please their own palates.

fried dates with almonds

These seductive Indian sweetmeats are fun to make when fresh dates are available. Prepare them ahead and fry shortly before serving. Date palms dot the landscape near Upington in the Northern Cape and an avenue of palms over a thousand metres long – one of the longest in the southern hemisphere – has been declared a National Monument.

makes 20

20 (about 400g) fresh dates
20 blanched almonds
Ghee (page 215) or butter

Slice into the dates, remove the seeds and press almonds into the hollows.

Fry in sizzling ghee or butter until brown and slightly crunchy. Drain on kitchen paper and serve cool.

almond kolwadjib

The name of this soft Malay sweetmeat is derived from the Malayan or Javanese gula-wajek. Some old recipes call them kowadjik, colvagied and koevagiep. If you wish, flossy up the presentation for special occasions with maraschino cherries and mint leaves.

makes about 24; serves 6 to 8

100g blanched almonds, finely chopped
50g desiccated coconut
750ml milk
finely grated zest of ½ orange
2ml ground cardamom
200g brown sugar
180g uncooked basmati rice
50g butter
2ml rose water

Lightly butter a 22cm square baking dish. Roast the almonds and coconut in a dry frying pan until well browned and aromatic. Allow to cool.

Pour the milk into a medium saucepan. Add the orange zest, cardamom and brown sugar. Heat, stirring, until the sugar dissolves. Stir in the rice, cover and simmer for about 20 minutes until the rice is very soft and the milk has been absorbed. Stir occasionally.

Remove from the heat. Stir in the butter and rose water, then mix in the roasted almonds and coconut. Spoon the mixture into the dish and press it down nice and level. Chill in the fridge for an hour or two. Cut into triangles and arrange on a tray.

carrot halwa

'Maharaja's gold' is a famous Indian pudding made with carrots, which are cheap, cheerful and plentiful. It's very sweet, so serve tiny portions.

serves 6 to 8

250g young carrots

50g flaked almonds

30g butter

250ml milk

100g sugar

2ml ground cardamom

silver dragees, for garnishing

Peel and coarsely grate the carrots. Roast the almonds in a dry frying pan until golden. Chop roughly.

Melt the butter in a large saucepan, add the carrots and fry over high heat for about 5 minutes until soft and lightly glazed.

Stir in the milk, sugar and cardamom, and simmer uncovered for about 10 minutes more until the carrots are very soft and the halwa is gorgeously thick and creamy. Stir occasionally; constantly towards the end to prevent the halwa from sticking to the pan.

Remove from the heat and mix in the almonds. Allow to cool, then spoon into small bowls or glasses and garnish with a pretty sprinkling of silver dragees.

it's fun to serve a variety of sweet-meats together so that everyone can help themselves to their favourites.

guavas in star anise syrup

Tropical fruit is abundant in Africa and is used in a variety of luscious puddings. Guavas, native to Mexico, Central America and parts of the Caribbean, are an important crop in South Africa, both for the fruit and the juice.

serves 6 to 8

1kg (12–14) ripe guavas
250ml white wine
125ml water
100g sugar
4 star anise
seeds scraped from 1 vanilla pod
1 stem lemongrass, lightly bruised
thin custard, to serve

Peel the guavas and cut in half. Combine the wine, water, sugar, star anise, vanilla and lemongrass in a large saucepan. Heat, stirring until the sugar dissolves. Cover and set aside for about 30 minutes for the flavours to infuse.

Add the guavas to the syrup, cover and simmer for 15 to 20 minutes until soft. The cooking time will depend on the ripeness of the fruit.

Lift the guavas into a bowl, pour over the syrup and allow to cool. Serve with custard.

port wine jellies

Birthday celebrations in the Cape Colony always ended with wine jelly served in tall glasses. Hout Bay fishermen, meanwhile, made a jelly called tschin-tschou set with lacy pink seaweed instead of gelatine. The seaweed was sun-dried, wrapped in muslin, boiled in water, strained and flavoured with sugar, vanilla essence, rose water and ground cardamom.

serves 4

500ml berry juice
60ml sugar
2 whole cloves
1 cinnamon stick
10g sachet powdered gelatine
100ml port
30ml lemon juice
sugared dried fruit, to serve

Combine the berry juice, sugar, cloves and cinnamon in a medium saucepan. Heat, stirring, until the sugar dissolves. Don't allow it to boil. Cover and set aside for about 15 minutes for the flavours of the spices to infuse.

Sprinkle the gelatine on the surface and allow it to sponge, then stir in until thoroughly dissolved. Add the port and lemon juice.

Strain the jelly mixture into a jug, then pour into glasses. Chill in the fridge to set; about 4 to 5 hours should do it. Pile with sugared dried fruit shortly before serving.

banana fritters

Fruit and vegetables dipped in batter and deep-fried are popular the world over, not least in Southeast Asia where you can purchase a variety of fritters from roadside vendors. Bananas make the best fritters of all, though they should be served shortly after frying. KwaZulu-Natal is banana country, where the fruit was first cultivated in the 1800s after an influx of Mauritian people had settled there.

serves 6

6 bananas
vegetable oil

BATTER
100g cake flour
50g cornflour
15ml castor sugar
15ml baking powder
1ml salt
200ml water (approximate amount)

Peel the bananas and cut into chunks.

BATTER Sift together the flour, cornflour, castor sugar, baking powder and salt. Mix in enough water to make a thickish coating batter.

Heat oil for deep-frying in a medium saucepan. Dip the banana chunks into the batter and deep-fry for a minute or two until crisp and golden. Drain on kitchen paper.

Pile the fritters on a plate and serve warm.

soft, LUSCIOUS PUMPKIN fritters are caLLeD 'BOLLaS' BY cape maLays.

pumpkin fritters with amaruLa cream

Pumpkin fritters are most often served for pudding, but are also delicious with curry or bobotie. Amarula Cream is a South African liqueur made from the fruit of the marula tree, which is also made into beer, jam and jelly. Any cream liqueur that takes your fancy may be substituted.

serves 4 to 6

FRITTERS
600g pumpkin
250ml water
1ml salt
1 egg, lightly beaten
100g cake flour
5ml baking powder
1ml ground cinnamon
1ml ground mace
vegetable oil

CINNAMON-SUGAR
60ml sugar
2ml ground cinnamon

AMARULA CREAM
250ml cream
60ml Amarula Cream liqueur

FRITTERS Skin the pumpkin, discard the pips and cut the flesh into cubes. Place in a medium saucepan with the water and salt. Cover and simmer for about 20 minutes until very soft. Drain well.

Mash the cooked pumpkin. Mix in the egg, flour, baking powder, cinnamon and mace.

Heat oil for deep-frying in a frying pan. Drop in spoonfuls of the batter and fry until golden on all sides. Drain on kitchen paper.

CINNAMON-SUGAR Mix the sugar and cinnamon together.

AMARULA CREAM Whip the cream to soft peaks. Fold in the liqueur.

Pile the pumpkin fritters onto a plate and sprinkle with cinnamon-sugar. Offer the amarula cream on the side.

pistachio nuts are popular in middle-eastern and indian dishes, and give khulfi a distinctive flavour and colour.

BOEBER

There are probably as many recipes for boeber as there are Cape Malay cooks! Some spell it boeboer, others bubur. Some offer it as a warm, spicy milk drink, others as a warm pudding. A similar Indian milk pudding, called doodh pak, is made either with vermicelli or basmati rice.

serves 6 to 8

45ml sago
1 litre milk
50g flaked almonds
50g butter
80g vermicelli, broken into pieces
1ml ground cardamom
1ml ground cinnamon
100g sugar
100g bleached sultanas
250ml cream
5ml vanilla extract

Place the sago in a small saucepan with 250ml of the milk. Bring to the boil, stirring continuously. Cover and set aside for 15 minutes for the sago to plump. Roast the almonds in a dry frying pan until golden. Allow to cool.

Melt the butter in a medium saucepan. Add the vermicelli, cardamom and cinnamon, and stir over very low heat until golden and aromatic.

Add the remaining milk, sugar, sultanas and sago, and cook over low heat for about 10 minutes until the vermicelli is tender and the sago is transparent. Stir occasionally at first, then constantly as the boeber thickens.

Remove from the heat and stir in the cream and vanilla extract. Spoon into bowls or glasses and sprinkle with roasted almonds.

KHULFI

Indian ice cream is the perfect way to end a spicy meal. Early recipes call for milk to be condensed by slowly simmering in a saucepan; a tin makes the task so much easier. This is a firm ice cream; remove from the freezer a little while before serving.

serves 8 to 10

500ml milk
60ml cornflour
100g blanched almonds, finely chopped
50g pistachio nuts, shelled and finely chopped
1ml ground cardamom
397g tin condensed milk
5ml vanilla extract or rose water

Measure 125ml of the milk into a jug and mix in the cornflour. Roast the almonds and pistachios in a dry frying pan until golden. Allow to cool.

Bring the remaining milk to the boil in a medium saucepan with the cardamom. Add the milk and cornflour mixture and boil for 2 to 3 minutes, stirring constantly, until thickened. Remove from the heat and stir in the condensed milk, nuts and vanilla extract or rose water.

Pour into a metal bowl and place in the freezer. Mix well every 30 minutes or so. After a few hours it will be too stiff for stirring, so re-whip with an electric beater until light and creamy. Re-freeze and repeat the whipping process a couple more times. Transfer the ice cream to a freezer-friendly container and freeze.

buttermilk pudding

After the first dairy was established in the mid-1600s, buttermilk became popular in the Cape. This is a very delicate custard so choose a wide baking dish rather than a deep one to bake in, and ensure that the water in the water bath comes as far as possible up the sides of the baking dish.

serves 6 to 8

50g soft butter, plus extra for the baking dish
150g castor sugar
4 eggs, separated
500ml buttermilk
5ml vanilla extract
60ml cake flour
1ml salt
500ml cream
honey, to serve

Heat the oven to 160°C. Lightly butter a wide baking dish. Cream together the butter and castor sugar. Beat in the egg yolks one by one, then mix in the buttermilk and vanilla extract. Sift the flour and salt onto the surface, and fold in gently.

Whip the cream until it holds soft peaks. Whip the egg whites stiffly. Mix both into the buttermilk base. Pour into the buttered baking dish.

Place the baking dish in a larger dish and pour in boiling water to come as far as possible up the sides. Bake uncovered for about 1 hour until the buttermilk pudding is cooked and doesn't wobble too much when you shake the dish.

Serve warm or cool with a drizzle of honey and extra whipped cream if you wish.

buttermilk pudding is south africa's light and luscious answer to france's famous crème caramel.

sago pudding

Early recipes for sago pudding called for honey as sweetener and rose water in place of vanilla extract. It's best served warm from the oven.

serves 6 to 8

200g sago

750ml milk

80g sugar

finely grated zest of 1 lemon

1ml salt

1ml grated nutmeg

50g butter, plus extra for the baking dish

125ml cream

5ml vanilla extract

2 egg yolks

50g flaked almonds

Heat the oven to 160°C. Butter a 2-litre oven-to-table baking dish, or 6 to 8 smaller dishes or cups for individual servings.

Combine the sago, milk, sugar, lemon zest, salt and nutmeg in a medium saucepan. Bring to the boil, stirring constantly. Remove from the heat and set aside for about 15 minutes for the sago to plump. Stir occasionally to distribute the sago evenly.

Beat in the butter, cream, vanilla extract and egg yolks. Pour into the baking dish/es and bake for about 45 minutes until set. The baking time for individual servings is 30 minutes.

Roast the almonds in a dry frying pan and sprinkle a few onto the pudding just before serving.

cape crème brûlée

The literal translation of crème brûlée is 'burnt custard' which refers to the crackly topping which, in bygone days, was done with a red-hot baker's shovel or branding iron. A blowtorch is today's caramelizer of choice; a piping hot oven griller will do almost as well. This version puts a local spin on things, with the addition of orange zest, cinnamon and a splash of Van der Hum. The original family recipe of this South African brandy-based liqueur was snaffled up by a wine merchant for the princely sum of 800 pounds. There were eventually twenty Van der Hum distillers in the Cape, one of whom is reported to have used 8000 baskets of naartjies every year for his brew; the amount of spices used (cloves, cinnamon, nutmeg and mace) is anyone's guess. Some say it was named after Admiral Van der Hum of the Dutch East India Company's fleet, who was particularly fond of it. If you can't find Van der Hum, use any citrus-based liqueur such as Cointreau, Curaçao or Grand Marnier.

serves 6

500ml cream

finely grated zest of ½ orange

2ml vanilla extract

45ml Van der Hum liqueur

5 egg yolks

60ml castor sugar

3 cinnamon sticks

brown sugar, for the topping

crème brûlée features in cookbooks from the eighteenth century and continues to seduce those who become misty-eyed and weak-kneed at the thought of it.

Heat the oven to 160°C. Combine the cream and orange zest in a medium saucepan and heat to just below boiling point. Remove from the heat and stir in the vanilla extract and Van der Hum.

Whisk the egg yolks and castor sugar together until well blended. Strain in the hot cream. Place six 125ml ramekins in a roasting tin and fill with the custard. Pour in boiling water to come halfway up the sides. Bake for about 50 minutes until the custard has set.

Break the cinnamon sticks in half and stick them into the custards. Cool to room temperature.

Shortly before serving, sprinkle a little brown sugar onto the custards and caramelize with a blowtorch.

CRÈME BRÛLÉE IS A
FABULOUS PUDDING —
SMOOTH, RICH CUSTARD
UNDER A CRISP SUGAR
TOPPING THAT GIVES way at
THE 'THWACK' OF A SPOON.

Bread and Butter Pudding

This comfort-zone favourite is as popular in Africa as it is in England, where the recipe originated. It's best made with bread that is past its prime. Some cooks add goodies like roasted almonds and candied orange rind, but there really is no need – though a dash of brandy or sherry perks things up, and a touch of spice such as ground cardamom adds Cape Malay flavour.

serves 6

butter
8 slices white bread
250g smooth apricot jam
100g bleached sultanas
500ml milk
5ml ground cinnamon
finely grated zest of 1 lemon
60ml sugar
10ml vanilla extract
3 eggs
30ml brandy or medium dry
    sherry (optional)
sugar
ground cinnamon

Butter a 2-litre oven-to-table dish. Butter the bread liberally and spread with jam. Cut into triangles and arrange in the baking dish, slices overlapping a little. Scatter sultanas between the slices, not on top (if they rise to the surface of the pud they may burn).

Combine the milk, cinnamon and lemon zest in a medium saucepan and heat to just below boiling point. Mix in the sugar, vanilla extract, eggs and brandy or sherry. Pour carefully into the dish (don't swish off all the jam) and set aside for about an hour to allow the liquid to soak in.

Meanwhile heat the oven to 160°C. Place the pudding dish in a larger baking dish, add boiling water to come halfway up the sides, and bake uncovered for 45 minutes until the custard has set.

Sprinkle a little sugar and cinnamon on the surface about 10 minutes before the end of the cooking time and increase oven temperature to 200°C to glaze the pudding. Serve warm.

malva pudding may be served from the baking dish or cut into squares, which will glam things up a bit.

malva pudding

Rumour has it that the curious name of this famous Cape Dutch dessert comes from malvasia, a sweet fortified wine that was the accompanying tipple of choice. But no record can be found of malvasia ever being made in South Africa. A more likely explanation is that 'marshmallow pudding' comes from its spongy texture. There are plenty of variations, some with less glamorous names like Vinegar Pudding and Telephone Pudding, which was how the recipe was passed from friend to friend.

serves 6

200g castor sugar

1 egg

15ml soft butter, plus extra
    for the baking dish

30ml smooth apricot jam

120g cake flour

5ml bicarbonate of soda

1ml salt

250ml milk

15ml wine vinegar

5ml vanilla extract

icing sugar, for sifting

softly whipped cream, to serve

SAUCE

250ml cream or evaporated milk

100g unsalted butter

125ml sugar

Heat the oven to 180°C. Butter a 2-litre oven-to-table baking dish.

Beat together the castor sugar, egg, butter and jam until pale and fluffy. Sift together the flour, bicarb and salt. Mix together the milk, vinegar and vanilla extract. Fold alternately into the egg mixture until thoroughly mixed. Pour the batter into the baking dish and bake for about 45 minutes until firm.

SAUCE While the pudding is baking, combine the sauce ingredients in a small saucepan. Heat, stirring, until the butter melts and the sugar has dissolved. Pour over the pudding as it comes out of the oven. Set aside for about 15 minutes to allow the pudding to absorb the sauce.

Serve warm from the baking dish, or cut into squares and arrange on a plate. Sift over a cloud of icing sugar and offer with whipped cream.

cape brandy pudding

Rich, yet light, syrupy and satisfying – perfect for when winter's chill settles in. This famous dish is named after brandy, which has been distilled in South Africa since 1672.

serves 8

250g dried pitted dates, chopped

250ml water

5ml bicarbonate of soda

100g soft butter, plus extra for
   the baking dish

170g castor sugar

1 egg

120g flour

5ml baking powder

1ml salt

100g pecan nuts or walnuts,
   roughly crumbled

250ml softly whipped cream, to serve

SYRUP

100g sugar

60ml water

60ml brandy

5ml vanilla extract

15ml butter

Heat the oven to 180°C. Butter a 2-litre oven-to-table baking dish. Combine the dates and water in a small saucepan and bring to the boil. Mix lightly. Remove from the heat, stir in the bicarb and allow to cool.

Cream together the butter, castor sugar and egg. Sift in the flour, baking powder and salt. Mix in lightly. Stir in the date mixture. Fold in the nuts. Pour into the baking dish and bake uncovered for 45 minutes until the pudding is firm.

SYRUP Combine the sugar and water in a small saucepan and bring to the boil, stirring to dissolve the sugar. Remove from the heat and mix in the brandy, vanilla extract and butter. Pour over the pudding as it comes out of the oven.

Serve warm with whipped cream.

PRACTISED HANDS ROLL DOUGH FOR ROTI, READY TO SPREAD WITH BUTTER. IT WILL THEN BE ROLLED UP AND ALLOWED TO REST BEFORE BEING ROLLED INTO ROUNDS AND FRIED.

BReaDS
& Home-Bakes
CHAPTER SEVENTEEN

BREAD-MAKING REFLECTS OUR DIVERSE COMMUNITIES – the dumplings of rural blacks, Malay roti, Cape Dutch wholewheat loaves, and Indian baked, fried and tandoori breads.

For early wandering pastoralists and trek-farmers, hollowed-out ant heaps made perfect baking ovens. Voortrekkers baked bread in their trusty three-legged potjies. Clay ovens – some large enough to accommodate forty loaves – came later. A fire was lit inside the door, then pushed to the back of the oven. After about an hour, the oven was hot enough. Fire and ash were raked out and bread pans of risen dough on long-handled broodskoppe (bread planks) were placed inside. The door was closed and sealed with clay.

Tribal folk baked in mud ovens – a hole in the ground with shelves to hold cakes and breads. And maize, sorghum and millet meal dumplings were steamed on sticks criss-crossed in water-filled clay pots. When communities became more settled, outside brick ovens were built. Later contraptions were modernized and brought indoors to the kitchen.

Early breads were made from flour crushed between stones powered by horses. Though unleavened, trace elements from the grinding stones impacted somewhat on the raising ability of the flour. Various pre-yeast raising agents included sourdough yeast made from hops and potatoes, and crushed raisins mixed with sugar and water. Palm wine was the standard raising agent of West Coast bread, and Karoo bakers used the root of a rare plant, which was considered superior even to yeast and baking powder.

Cake baking for the tea-time scene came into its own after Britain usurped Holland as rulers of the Cape Colony in the early 1800s. Rather than reflect any intrinsic South African character, however, cakes and tarts echoed fashionable European trends of the time.

The best way to judge our enthusiasm for sweet things and baking skills is to attend a fête, festival or family celebration. The array of delicious goodies gaily decorated with glacé and sugared fruit, silver dragees, whipped cream, nuts and coconut speaks for itself – and of folk who take pleasure in baking up a storm whenever they have the chance.

PURI

These unleavened flatbreads are found throughout India and Malaysia, and are made from a simple dough of flour, oil, water and salt which is fried in ghee or oil. The idea is to break off bits to scoop up mouthfuls of curry, rice, lentils or beans. They're best served straight from the pan while still wonderfully crisp and puffed up with air.

makes 8

120g cake flour
2ml salt
30ml vegetable oil, plus extra for frying
100ml water (approximate amount)

Sift the flour and salt into a bowl. Mix in the oil, then add enough water to make a soft dough. Turn out onto a floured surface and knead for about 10 minutes until smooth and elastic.

Divide the dough into eight and roll out thinly into rounds on a floured surface. Deep-fry the puri in oil until puffed, crisp and golden – hold them under the oil if they rise to the surface. Drain on kitchen paper and serve warm.

roti

Roti are crisp, flaky and rich with butter; the perfect accompaniment for curry. It's worth making a lot, as the dough keeps well in the fridge and the roti can be fried as required.

makes about 12, depending on size

180g cake flour
2ml salt
20ml vegetable oil, plus extra for frying
150ml water (approximate amount)
40g very soft butter

Sift the flour and salt into a large bowl. Mix in the oil, then add enough water to make a soft dough. Turn out onto a floured surface and knead for about 10 minutes until smooth and elastic.

Roll the dough out to about 24cm x 36cm. Spread with soft butter and roll up. Cover with a cloth and set aside to rest for about 30 minutes.

Cut the roll into 12 slices (depending on the size of the roti you wish to make) and roll into balls between your palms. Roll out on a floured surface and stack interleaved with waxed paper.

Fry the roti in hot oil until pale golden and crisp on each side. Drain on kitchen paper and serve warm.

vetkoek

These delightful old-fashioned goodies – literally translated as 'fat cakes' – have filled many an empty tummy. Bits of bread dough were pinched off, allowed to rise and deep-fried in dripping. Serve vetkoek at a braai with a little salt, or break them open and fill with a savoury filling. They're also bliss sprinkled with cinnamon-sugar or drizzled with honey, syrup or jam as a tea-time treat.

serves 6

300g cake flour
10g sachet instant dried yeast
15ml sugar
5ml salt
15ml wine vinegar
15ml vegetable oil, plus extra for frying
250ml warm water (approximate amount)

Sift the flour, yeast, sugar and salt into a bowl. Mix in the vinegar and oil, then add enough warm water to form a soft dough. Transfer to an oiled bowl, cover and set aside in a warm spot until doubled in bulk.

Heat oil for deep-frying in a large saucepan. Break off bits of risen dough and fry for 5 to 6 minutes until golden and cooked through, turning frequently. Drain well on kitchen paper and serve warm.

white bread

There's nothing quite like the smell of baking bread, whether it's being baked in the oven or a cast-iron pot nestled in the coals. A story which did the rounds in the 1890s claimed that the value of 'delicately nurtured' girls visiting their brothers in the African wilds (presumably to add feminine touches to the rough life of far-flung outposts of the Empire) were judged entirely on their bread-making skills.

makes 1 Large Loaf

500g cake flour

5ml salt

20g (2 sachets) instant dried yeast

5ml sugar

30g butter, cut into small blocks

300ml warm milk

1 egg yolk, lightly beaten

Grease a large loaf tin. Sift the flour, salt, yeast and sugar into a bowl. Mix the butter into the warm milk, pour into the dry ingredients and mix to a firm dough.

Turn onto a floured surface and knead for about 10 minutes until smooth and elastic. Place in a lightly oiled bowl, cover with a cloth and place in a warm spot until doubled in bulk.

Punch the dough down and knead lightly. Form into small balls and pack into the loaf tin – they should come about halfway up the side. Place in a warm, draught-free spot for about 30 minutes until the dough has risen to the edges of the tin. Heat the oven to 180°C.

Brush the dough with egg yolk and bake for 15 minutes. Reduce the oven heat to 160°C and bake for a further 30 minutes until done and the loaf sounds hollow when tapped. Turn out onto a wire rack to cool.

To make Roosterkoek (bread rolls cooked over the coals), prepare the white bread dough and shape into small balls between your palms. Set aside until doubled in size. Place on the grid and braai over low coals. As soon as the underside is crisp, turn carefully and cook until they sound hollow when tapped. Cool, then split and serve with butter.

maize bread

Maize makes delicious bread, whether you use the meal or corn kernels or both, as in this recipe. It's delicious sliced and buttered and offered with grated cheese.

makes 1 small Loaf

250g cake flour

10ml baking powder

5ml salt

60g maize meal

340g tin whole kernel corn

3 eggs

175ml plain yoghurt

Heat the oven to 200°C. Grease a small loaf tin. Sift the flour, baking powder and salt into a bowl. Mix in the maize meal. Drain the corn, and mix in.

Beat together the eggs and yoghurt and mix in. Pour into the loaf tin and bake for about 1¼ hours until the bread is cooked and a skewer comes out clean. Turn out onto a wire rack to cool.

buttermilk rusks are an afrikaner biscuit, created for snacking during treks around the country in days gone by.

buttermilk rusks

Karringmelkbeskuit are perfect snacks for any time of the day. They're especially hard to beat when dipped into coffee first thing in the morning.

makes 32

750g self-raising flour
5ml salt
100g sugar
200g soft butter, cut into cubes
500ml buttermilk
2 eggs, lightly beaten

Grease and lightly flour two small loaf tins. Heat the oven to 160°C. Lightly flour your worktop.

Sift together the flour, salt and sugar. Rub in the butter until the mixture is crumbly. Mix together the buttermilk and eggs and add enough to bring the flour together. Knead for a minute or two until you have a soft dough.

Roll out with your hands to a fat sausage and divide into 16 balls. Pack into the prepared loaf tins; they should come about two-thirds of the way to the rim.

Bake for 30 minutes. Reduce the oven heat to 120°C and bake for a further 30 minutes. Remove the half-baked rusks from the tins, break them apart and break each one in half. Arrange on baking trays and return the rusks to the oven for 3 to 4 hours more to dry. Cool in the oven. Store in an airtight container.

karamonk biscuits

These spicy Malay biscuits are traditionally flavoured with cardamom and ground, dried naartjie (tangerine) peel. Finely grated orange zest works just as well.

makes about 40

100g soft butter
30ml vegetable oil
100g sugar
1 egg, lightly beaten
120g cake flour
2ml baking powder
1ml salt
2ml ground cardamom
2ml ground cinnamon
10ml finely grated orange zest
80g desiccated coconut
glacé orange peel or glacé cherries
    for decoration (optional)

Heat the oven to 160°C. Cream together the butter, oil and sugar until light and fluffy. Beat in the egg. Sift in the flour, baking powder, salt, cardamom, cinnamon and orange zest, and mix in. Add the coconut and mix to a fairly soft dough.

Roll the dough into small balls between floured palms. Place on lightly greased baking trays and press lightly. Allow plenty of space between each for spreading. Decorate with pieces of glacé orange peel or cherries if you wish. Bake for 12 to 15 minutes until golden. Cool on wire racks and store in an airtight container.

hertzog koekies

Cape Malay hertzoggies (as they're fondly known) are served at any party you'd care to mention – celebratory teas, weddings and Eid.

makes 12

SHORTCRUST PASTRY
250g cake flour

50g icing sugar

1ml salt

150g cold unsalted butter,
   cut into small cubes

1 egg

FILLING
450g tin smooth apricot jam

2 egg whites

100g castor sugar

2ml vanilla extract

50g desiccated coconut

SHORTCRUST PASTRY Sift together the flour, icing sugar and salt. Rub in the butter until the mixture in finely crumbled. Add the egg and mix until the dough comes together. Wrap the pastry in waxed paper and refrigerate for about 30 minutes.

Heat the oven to 200°C. Roll the pastry out on a floured surface and cut into rounds to line 24 muffin pans. Prick the bases and bake for about 12 minutes until pale golden in colour. Cool.

FILLING Reduce the oven heat to 180°C. Fill the tarts with apricot jam. Beat the egg whites to stiff peaks. Add the castor sugar little by little, beating well after each addition. Beat in the vanilla extract. Fold in the coconut.

Spoon or pipe the coconut meringue onto the jam and bake the tarts for about 20 minutes until the meringue is crisp. Cool for a few minutes in the pans, then lift out and cool on a wire rack.

hertzog koekies were a cape malay creation in honour of general jbm hertzog, first prime minister of the union of south africa between 1924 and 1939, after he promised to give women the vote.

tangy Lemon curd — from the seventeenth century curd tarts of europe — has topped many a slice of toast and filled plenty of pastry cases.

Lemon curd tarts

It's a good idea to make extra lemon curd while you're at it to bottle and keep in the fridge. For orange curd, use orange zest and juice instead of lemon, but as oranges are sweeter, reduce the sugar by half.

makes 10 to 12

LEMON CURD

3 egg yolks

100g castor sugar

finely grated zest of 2 medium lemons

125ml lemon juice

5ml cornflour

60g butter, cut into small cubes

LEMON SHORTCRUST PASTRY

250g cake flour

60g icing sugar

125g cold unsalted butter, cut into small cubes

finely grated zest of 1 lemon

2ml vanilla extract

1 egg, lightly beaten

LEMON CRISPS

2 lemons

icing sugar

LEMON CURD Place the egg yolks and castor sugar into a saucepan and whisk off the heat until well blended. Mix in the lemon zest and juice and cornflour, and cook over low heat, stirring constantly, until the mixture thickens like custard and coats the spoon.

Remove from the heat. Whisk in the diced butter and chill.

LEMON SHORTCRUST PASTRY Sift together the flour and icing sugar. Rub in the butter until the mixture is finely crumbled. Add the lemon zest and vanilla extract and mix in lightly. Add the egg and knead until the dough comes together. Wrap in waxed paper and chill for 30 minutes.

Heat the oven to 180°C. Grease 10 to 12 6cm cake tins. Roll out the pastry and cut into circles to line the tins. Prick the bases and bake for about 12 minutes until the pastry is crisp and pale golden in colour.

Allow the pastry cases to cool. Fill with lemon curd and decorate with lemon crisps shortly before serving.

LEMON CRISPS Heat the oven to 200°C. Slice the lemons finely. Arrange on a greased baking tray and sift a little icing sugar over. Bake for about 10 minutes until crisp.

koeksisters

In the late 1700s the worth of a wife was measured by the quality of her koeksisters – syrupy Batavian delectations which are our most popular (and fattening!) treats. One enthusiastic koeksister-maker was affectionately nicknamed Betje Bolletjie because of her extraordinary skills, and she sold her wares far and wide. The odd name is believed to have come from two eccentric Dutch sisters who first had the notion to plait their doughnuts, little knowing they would be immortalized. The secret of success is in the preparation. If possible, make both syrup and dough a day ahead; the syrup should be well chilled and the dough well rested. Deep-fry the koeksisters as soon as possible after plaiting, and dip into syrup while still hot. Store lightly covered on a tray – not in an airtight container, or they'll lose their crackly crunch.

makes about 36

SYRUP

500ml water

1kg sugar

2ml cream of tartar

2ml ground ginger

finely grated zest and
   juice of 1 lemon

DOUGH

500g cake flour

30ml baking powder

2ml salt

50g butter, cut into small cubes

1 egg

250ml milk

vegetable oil

SYRUP Combine the ingredients in a large saucepan and bring to the boil, stirring until the sugar dissolves. Boil without stirring for about 5 minutes to form a light syrup. Strain into a large bowl, cool then refrigerate until well chilled.

DOUGH Sift together the flour, baking powder and salt. Rub in the butter until the mixture is finely crumbled. Whisk the egg with 200ml of the milk, add to the flour mixture and knead to make a soft, pliable dough. Add the remaining milk only if the dough is too stiff. Form into a ball, wrap in waxed paper and chill for a couple of hours; overnight if possible.

Roll the dough out on a lightly floured surface to a thickness of 1cm. Cut into oblongs 8cm x 4cm, and cut each into three strips almost to the top. Plait together and pinch the ends tightly to seal. Place on a tray and cover with a damp cloth.

Deep-fry a few koeksisters at a time in hot oil, turning constantly. Watch the heat: they take 2 to 3 minutes to cook through and turn golden brown. Drain briefly on kitchen paper, then dip while still hot into cold syrup. (If it warms up, place the syrup in a larger bowl of cold water with ice blocks.) Drain the excess syrup back into the bowl and drain the koeksisters on a rack.

these cape malay treats are plumper, spongier and spicier than the plaited koeksisters (spelt with an extra 'k').

koesisters

On Sunday mornings in the 'good old days', koesisters were hawked by District Six children, to passers-by. Another type of koesister was made with cooked potato, a recipe created by Mrs Samsodien of Hanover Street, when there was a shortage of flour during the Second World War. Koesisters are best eaten within a few hours of being fried.

makes about 15, depending on size

250g cake flour
60ml castor sugar
1ml salt
5g (10ml) instant dried yeast
5ml ground ginger
5ml ground cinnamon
5ml ground aniseed
2ml ground cardamom
60ml vegetable oil, plus extra
    for frying
1 egg
50ml milk
50ml water
desiccated coconut, for sprinkling

SYRUP

500ml water
200g sugar
1ml bicarbonate of soda
10g butter

Sift together the flour, castor sugar, salt, yeast and spices into a bowl. Lightly mix together the oil and egg, and mix into the dry ingredients. Mix together the milk and water in a small saucepan and heat to blood temperature. Mix in to form a soft dough. Place in an oiled bowl, cover with a cloth and set aside in a warm spot until doubled in bulk. This will take about 2 hours, depending on the weather.

Roll the dough out with your hands on a lightly oiled surface into a sausage about 5cm thick. Cut into 2cm lengths, form into flattened doughnut shapes and arrange on a tray; leave space for rising. Cover with a cloth and set aside for about 30 minutes until doubled in size.

SYRUP   Bring the water and sugar to the boil in a large saucepan, stirring until the sugar dissolves. Boil uncovered until reduced by half and thickened to a light syrup. Stir in the bicarb and butter.

Deep-fry the koesisters in medium-hot oil for about 5 minutes, turning constantly, until golden, crisp and cooked through. Drain briefly on kitchen paper. Drop into the syrup and simmer gently for about 30 minutes. Lift onto a serving plate and sprinkle with coconut.

cupcakes

Cupcakes or Fairy Cakes – individual cakes perfect for children's parties – are so named because they're about the size of a teacup.

makes 24

250g soft butter

300g castor sugar

2ml vanilla extract

4 eggs

450g self-raising flour

2ml salt

250ml milk

BUTTER ICING

250g soft butter

500g icing sugar, sifted

2ml vanilla extract

food colouring (optional)

Heat the oven to 180°C. Place paper cupcake holders in 24 muffin pans.

Cream together the butter and castor sugar until pale and fluffy. Mix in the vanilla extract. Add the eggs one by one, beating well after each addition.

Sift together the flour and salt, and fold in gently with the milk. Spoon the batter into the cupcake papers and bake for 12 to 15 minutes until golden. Allow to cool.

BUTTER ICING Beat the butter with an electric beater until pale and doubled in volume. Add the icing sugar little by little, beating well after each addition. Add the vanilla extract. Divide the icing in half and add different food colourings to each. Pipe prettily onto the cupcakes and decorate with sifted icing sugar and silver dragees.

CHILDREN OF ALL AGES ADORE CUPCAKES, ESPECIALLY WHEN THEY'RE FLOSSIED UP WITH OUTRAGEOUS ICING.

meLkteRt

East meets West in this famous Dutch milk tart, which is usually baked in an enamel dish. In summer, pastry would be made in the cool of the night and baked before sunrise. The custard was flavoured with dried naartjie (tangerine) peel, blanched almonds and peach kernels. Coconut milk or sweet wine were sometimes added.

serves 8

500g puff pastry
500ml milk
3 eggs, separated
80ml cake flour
15ml cornflour
80ml castor sugar
2ml baking powder
2ml ground cinnamon
30g butter
5ml vanilla extract

Heat the oven to 200°C. Lightly grease a 24cm shallow enamel bowl or baking tin. Unroll the pastry and line the baking tin. Press a piece of lightly oiled foil into the pastry and bake for 10 minutes. Remove the foil and bake the crust for about 5 minutes more until lightly browned and crisp. Allow to cool.

Measure 400ml of the milk into a saucepan. Mix together the remaining milk, egg yolks, flour, cornflour, castor sugar, baking powder and cinnamon. Pour into the saucepan and cook, stirring, until the custard thickens. Remove from the heat and whisk in the butter and vanilla extract. Cool to room temperature.

Reduce the oven heat to 180°C. Whisk the egg whites to stiff peaks and fold into the custard. Pour into the pastry shell and bake for 10 minutes. Reduce the oven heat to 160°C and bake for about 30 minutes more until the filling has set. Serve warm.

Lemon meringue pie

This fabulous pie is a favourite for afternoon tea, and pops up regularly at farm stalls, fêtes and farmers' markets. Remember to use only full-cream condensed milk and the juice of yellow lemons, otherwise the filling may not set.

serves 12

BISCUIT CRUST

100g brazil nuts, finely chopped

200g crunchy biscuits, crushed

60g desiccated coconut

125g butter, melted

FILLING

2 x 397g tins full-cream condensed milk

4 eggs, separated

200ml freshly squeezed lemon juice

30ml castor sugar

BISCUIT CRUST Heat the oven to 180°C. Mix together the nuts, biscuit crumbs and coconut. Mix in the butter and press into a deep, 24cm loose-based baking tin. Bake for about 10 minutes until lightly browned. Allow to cool.

FILLING Mix together the condensed milk, egg yolks and lemon juice. Pour into the crust and chill for a couple of hours until set.

Just before serving, preheat the oven griller. Whip the egg whites to stiff peaks. Beat in the castor sugar until the mixture is stiff and glossy. Pile on top of the tart to form peaks and brown under the griller – watch carefully, it burns in a flash!

carrot cake

Carrots and beetroot have been used in cakes since medieval times, and this moist, dense cake has been popular for as long as any of us can remember.

makes 1 Large cake

4 eggs
200g castor sugar
200g butter, melted
125ml milk
5ml vanilla extract
300g cake flour
10ml baking powder
5ml bicarbonate of soda
5ml ground cinnamon
2ml salt
1ml ground allspice
300g carrots, grated or finely chopped
100g walnuts

ICING
250ml cream
250g cream cheese
30ml castor sugar
5ml vanilla extract

Heat the oven to 180°C. Grease and flour a 26cm loose-based ring tin or cake tin.

Cream together the eggs and castor sugar until pale and fluffy. Mix together the melted butter, milk and vanilla extract, and mix in. Sift together the flour, baking powder, bicarb, cinnamon, salt and allspice and fold in. Mix in the carrots. Roughly crumble most of the walnuts (leave a few for garnishing) and mix in. Pour into the cake tin.

Bake for 40 minutes (if using a ring tin); 60 minutes (if using a cake tin). Test with a skewer – it should come out clean. Turn out the cake onto a rack and cool.

ICING   Whip the cream stiffly. Beat in the cream cheese, castor sugar and vanilla extract. Pile the icing onto the cake and garnish with walnuts.

queen of sheba cake

This gloriously decadent cake is an adaptation of a famous Victorian cake which was introduced to South Africa by British settlers.

serves 10 to 12

100g soft butter
120g castor sugar
3 eggs, separated
200g dark chocolate, roughly chopped
100g ground almonds
15ml cocoa powder
15ml cake flour
2ml baking powder
30ml orange juice
15ml orange liqueur
5ml vanilla extract
10ml finely grated orange zest
1ml salt
1ml cream of tartar
strawberries, to garnish

Heat the oven to 160°C. Grease and line a 20cm loose-based cake tin. Cream together the butter and castor sugar until pale and fluffy. Add the egg yolks one by one, mixing well each time.

Melt the chocolate in a bowl over simmering water. Mix until smooth and stir into the egg mixture with the ground almonds.

Sift in the cocoa powder, flour and baking powder and fold in with the orange juice, liqueur, vanilla extract and orange zest.

Beat the egg whites stiffly with the salt and cream of tartar. Fold into the batter. Pour into the cake tin and bake for about 45 minutes until the cake is cooked and a skewer comes out clean. Loosen the edges and place on a rack to cool in the tin. Unmould, place on a plate and garnish with strawberries.

CHOCOLATE cake

This moist, rich chocolate cake has a traditional filling made with dates and nuts, though you're welcome to fill it with extra chocolate cream icing if you prefer.

SERVES 12

250g self-raising flour
300g castor sugar
2ml salt
5ml bicarbonate of soda
60ml cocoa powder
125g butter
300ml milk
5ml vanilla extract
2 eggs

DATE AND NUT FILLING

30ml cocoa powder
125ml sugar
125ml water
15g butter
125g dried or fresh pitted dates, finely chopped
15ml cornflour
30ml port
50g finely chopped walnuts or pecan nuts

CHOCOLATE CREAM ICING

200g soft butter
200g icing sugar, sifted
60g cocoa powder
1 egg, lightly beaten
5ml vanilla extract

Heat the oven to 170°C. Grease and flour a 23cm loose-based ring tin. Sift together the flour, castor sugar, salt, bicarb and cocoa.

Melt the butter and lightly whisk in the milk, vanilla extract and eggs. Mix into the dry ingredients. Pour the batter into the cake tin and bake for about 45 minutes until the cake is cooked and a skewer comes out clean. Turn out onto a cake rack to cool.

DATE AND NUT FILLING Mix together the cocoa, sugar, water, butter and dates in a small saucepan. Heat, while mashing the dates with a fork. Simmer uncovered until thick and smooth, stirring occasionally. Mix together the cornflour and port, add and stir until the mixture thickens. Allow to cool. Stir in the nuts.

CHOCOLATE CREAM ICING Beat all the ingredients together until well blended.

Cut the cake into two layers, sandwich together with the date and nut filling and cover the top and sides with chocolate cream icing. Decorate, if you wish, with blanched almonds and mint sprigs.

the african kitchen relies heavily on freshly-made masalas, which are so much more pungent than ready-made store-bought mixes.

the african pantry

CHAPTER EIGHTEEN

Roasted masala

Roasted masala has many uses besides as a replacement for curry powder. It's also great to spice up red meat, chicken or fish before roasting, grilling or braaiing.

makes about 350g

150g coriander seeds

125g cumin seeds

2 cinnamon sticks, broken into small pieces

5g whole cloves

20g cardamom pods, lightly crushed

25g crushed black peppercorns

25g turmeric

25g ground ginger

25g crushed dried chillies

Place the coriander, cumin, cinnamon, cloves and cardamom in a dry frying pan and roast, tossing lightly until aromatic. Remove from the heat and mix in the pepper, turmeric, ginger and dried chillies.

Grind as finely as possible with a pestle and mortar or spice grinder. Sieve, then grind the coarser bits once more. Discard the coarsest bits of spicing. Store in a screw-topped jar in a cool cupboard, or in the fridge or freezer.

green masala

A wide range of commercial masalas and spicings are available, but there's nothing to touch home-made mixtures, which can vary depending on personal preference. And there's something wonderfully sensual about grinding, roasting and mixing your own spices to make purées, pastes and powders. For red masala, simply substitute green chillies with red.

makes 200g

100g green chillies, washed and trimmed

50g green ginger, peeled

30g garlic cloves

45ml vegetable oil, plus extra for covering

2ml turmeric

45ml water

Pound the ingredients to a paste in a pestle and mortar, or whizz in a blender or food processor. Bottle and chill in the fridge, where it may be stored for a couple of months. Pour in a little vegetable oil to cover the surface.

garam masala

The word garam (or gharum) means 'warm' or 'hot'. Always add garam masala at the end of the cooking time to retain the fresh flavour.

makes about 130g

15g whole cloves
25g cumin seeds
25g coriander seeds
25g crushed black peppercorns
30g cardamom pods, lightly crushed
2 cinnamon sticks, broken into small pieces

Combine the ingredients a dry frying pan and roast, tossing lightly until aromatic. Grind as finely as possible with a pestle and mortar or spice grinder. Sieve, then grind the coarser bits once more. Discard the coarsest bits of spicing. Store in a screw-topped jar in a cool cupboard, or in the fridge or freezer.

berbere paste

Berbere (or berbiri) means 'hot sauce' and this magical paste is a traditional Ethiopian flavouring, with paprika as the dominant spice.

makes about 60mL

10ml cumin seeds

6 whole cloves

5ml cardamom pods, lightly crushed

5ml coriander seeds

1 red chilli, seeded and chopped

4 garlic cloves

20g green ginger, peeled and chopped

30ml paprika

2ml turmeric

2ml ground cinnamon

2ml milled black pepper

Roast the cumin, cloves, cardamom and coriander in a dry frying pan. Grind with a pestle and mortar or spice grinder. Add the chilli, garlic and ginger and continue grinding to a fine paste. Mix in the paprika, turmeric, cinnamon and pepper. Bottle and store in the fridge.

ghee

Clarified butter is the very best for frying, as it may be heated to a very high temperature without burning. Keep chilled and use as required.

makes about 350g

500g butter

Place the butter in a deep saucepan and boil gently uncovered for about 10 minutes. It will bubble as the water evaporates, and a layer of scum will rise to the surface. Remove from the heat, scoop off the scum and pour off the clear ghee, leaving the layer of salt at the bottom. Cool and store in the fridge.

fish stock

The quality of fish stock depends entirely on the quality and freshness of the fish bones used. White fish is best; don't use salmon or oily fish. Don't use the gills and wash everything well to make sure there are no traces of blood, as this will make the stock bitter and cloudy.

makes about 1 Litre

1kg white fish heads and bones
 (discard gills and entrails)
1,2 litres cold water
250ml dry white wine
½ onion, roughly chopped
1 carrot, roughly chopped
1 celery stick with leaves, roughly chopped
1 bunch parsley
1 lemon, sliced
12 black peppercorns

Combine the ingredients in a large saucepan, cover and bring to the boil. Reduce the heat and simmer very, very gently for 20 minutes.

Allow the stock to settle for about 30 minutes then drain into a bowl through a colander lined with muslin or 'kitchen wipes'. Chill or freeze.

chicken stock

If you don't have a chicken carcass to make stock with, purchase drumsticks, thighs or wings instead.

makes about 1 Litre

2 litres cold water
1 raw chicken carcass, with trimmings and giblets
 (not the liver)
4 leeks, roughly sliced
1 celery stick with leaves, roughly chopped
1 carrot, roughly chopped
1 bunch of herbs (parsley, thyme, bay leaf)
2ml black peppercorns

Combine all the ingredients in a large saucepan, cover and bring to the boil. Reduce the heat and simmer very gently for 2 to 3 hours. Strain into a clean saucepan.

Check the flavour; you might like to concentrate the stock by boiling uncovered for awhile. Chill or freeze.

beef stock

This is a standard recipe for veal, beef, lamb or venison stock. Vary the bones accordingly.

makes about 500mL

- 1,5kg veal, beef, lamb or venison bones
- 2 onions, quartered
- 2 carrots, quartered
- 3 celery sticks with leaves, roughly chopped
- 125ml vegetable oil
- 250ml dry red wine
- 2 litres cold water
- 1 bunch of herbs (parsley, thyme, bay leaf)

Heat the oven to 200°C. Place the bones in a roaster with the onions, carrots and celery. Pour over the oil, mix in lightly and roast uncovered for about 3 hours until well browned. Turn the ingredients occasionally so they roast evenly.

Transfer the bones and vegetables to a large saucepan. Pour the wine into the roaster and stir to deglaze. Add to the saucepan with the water and herbs. Cover and simmer gently for 3 to 4 hours.

Strain the stock into a clean saucepan and boil uncovered until reduced by two-thirds and well flavoured.

metric conversion chart

Metric measurements have been given in this book. Conversion to standard US and imperial measures are given below. Please remember that the equivalents are not exact, as measurements have been rounded out. Use either metric or imperial measurements, but not a mixture of both.

VOLUME AND LIQUID MEASURES

1 litre	4 cups
750ml	3 cups
500ml	2 cups
375ml	1½ cups
300ml	1¼ cups
250ml	1 cup
200ml	¾ cup
150ml	⅔ cup
125ml	½ cup
80ml	⅓ cup
60ml	¼ cup
45ml	3 tablespoons
30ml	2 tablespoons
20ml	4 teaspoons
15ml	1 tablespoon
10ml	2 teaspoons
7ml	1½ teaspoons
5ml	1 teaspoon
2ml	½ teaspoon
1ml	¼ teaspoon

WEIGHTS

900g	2lbs
450g	1lb
270g	9oz
230g	8oz
200g	7oz
180g	6oz
140g	5oz
115g	4oz
90g	3oz
60g	2oz
30g	½oz

OVEN TEMPERATURES

Deg C	Deg F	Gas
100	200	1
120	250	1
140	275	2
160	325	2
180	350	3
200	400	4
220	450	5–6

recipe index

ACKNOWLEDGEMENTS

Chris Bradburn of **Clay Café** for the hand-crafted plates and
bowls that augmented the Snyman family's stock of crockery used
in the photographs.

Gold Restaurant in Cape Town and the **Neighbourgoods Market**
in Woodstock for providing the locations for some of the photography.

LANNICE SNYMAN PUBLISHERS

First Published in 2008
PO Box 26344, Hout Bay 7872, South Africa
E-mail: lannice@lannicesnyman.com
Website: www.lannicesnyman.com

Author: Lannice Snyman
Design: PETALDESIGN
Cover Design: Matthew Ibbotson @ PETALDESIGN
Picture Research: Jenna Zetisky @ PETALDESIGN
Food Photographer: Warren Heath
Photographic Assistant: Juanita van Wyk
Food Stylist: Tamsin Snyman
Kitchen Assistant and Braaier: Courtenay Snyman
Proofreader: Joy Clack

ADDITIONAL PHOTOGRAPHY

Gallo Images: pages 11 (bottom), 26, 29 (top left; top right), 30 (left),
50, 70, 74 (top left; top right), 75, 90, 93 (left), 94, 95, 122, 125, 126 (right),
140, 149, 150 (bottom), 162 & 165 (right)
Images of Africa: pages 8, 11 (top right) & 12
Lannice Snyman: pages 54 (top left; top right), 73 (bottom), 74 (bottom)
& 93 (right)
Tamsin Snyman: pages 14, 15 (right), 53 (top centre), 54 (bottom right),
93 (right), 165 (left) & 166
Neil Corder: pages 47 (bottom left), 53 (top left) & 87 (bottom centre)
Craig Fraser: page 30 (right centre)
Tara Fisher: page 30 (top right)
Matthew Ibbotson: page 53 (top right; bottom)
Roy Zetisky: page 73 (top left; top right)
Jenna Zetisky: page 29 (bottom)
Capespirit.com: page 54 (bottom left)
Anthony Friend: page 30 (bottom)
Dennis Barling: page 6 & rally photographs

Pre-Press Production: Resolution Colour (Pty) Ltd, Cape Town
Printed and Binding: Tien Wah Press (Pte) Limited, Singapore
ISBN 978-0-620-41993-2